MW00466770

THEIR TROTSKY AND OURS

Their Trotsky and Ours

JACK BARNES

Pathfinder

NEW YORK   LONDON   MONTREAL   SYDNEY

Edited by Steve Clark and Mary-Alice Waters

Copyright © 1983, 2002 Pathfinder Press
All rights reserved

ISBN 0-87348-955-1
Library of Congress Control Number: 2002109556
Manufactured in the United States of America

First edition, 2002

COVER DESIGN: Eric Simpson
COVER PAINTING: Robert Motherwell, *The Garden Window (Open No. 110)*,
1969. 60 1/4 x 40 1/8 x 2 inches, acrylic on canvas. Collection of the Modern
Art Museum of Fort Worth, Museum Purchase, The Friends of Art
Endowment Fund. © Dedalus Foundation, Inc. / Licensed by VAGA, New
York, NY.

Pathfinder

410 West Street, New York, NY 10014, U.S.A.
www.pathfinderpress.com
E-mail: pathfinderpress@compuserve.com
Fax: (212) 727-0150

PATHFINDER DISTRIBUTORS AROUND THE WORLD:
Australia (and Southeast Asia and the Pacific):
    Pathfinder, Level 1, 3/281-287 Beamish St., Campsie, NSW 2194
    Postal address: P.O. Box 164, Campsie, NSW 2194
Canada:
    Pathfinder, 2761 Dundas St. West, Toronto, ON, M6P 1Y4
Iceland:
    Pathfinder, Skolavordustig 6B, Reykjavík
    Postal address: P. Box 0233, IS 121 Reykjavík
New Zealand:
    Pathfinder, P.O. Box 3025, Auckland
Sweden:
    Pathfinder, Domargränd 16, S-129 47 Hägersten
United Kingdom (and Europe, Africa, Middle East, and South Asia):
    Pathfinder, 47 The Cut, London, SE1 8LL
United States (and Caribbean, Latin America, and East Asia):
    Pathfinder, 410 West Street, New York, NY 10014

Contents

About the author

JACK BARNES has been national secretary of the Socialist Workers Party since 1972. He is also a contributing editor to *New International*, a magazine of Marxist politics and theory, and the author of many books, pamphlets, and articles.

An organizer of the Fair Play for Cuba Committee and actions in defense of Black rights, Barnes joined the Young Socialist Alliance in 1960 and the Socialist Workers Party in 1961. In 1965 he was elected national chairperson of the Young Socialist Alliance and became the director of the SWP and YSA's work in the growing movement against the Vietnam War. He has been a member of the National Committee of the Socialist Workers Party since 1963 and a national officer of the party since 1969. He has carried major responsibilities for the party's international work for almost forty years.

Beginning in the mid-1970s Barnes led the political turn of the Socialist Workers Party toward opportunities to get the overwhelming majority of its members and leaders into the industrial working class and unions. From that base, party members have built the communist movement while actively engaged with fellow workers in efforts to transform the unions into revolutionary instruments of struggle that defend not only their own membership but the interests of workers and farmers worldwide. The 1978–91 record of this work is published in *The Changing Face of U.S. Politics*.

Since 1998 Barnes has led the campaign of the SWP and fraternal organizations internationally to build on those advances, responding to openings created by the toughening resistance and actions by vanguard layers of workers and farmers standing up to the bosses' drive to increase profits on the backs of the producers. The opening of this political effort, and of the adjustments the party is making in its organizational forms among working people engaged in these struggles, is recorded in "A Sea Change in Working-Class Politics," the first chapter of *Capitalism's World Disorder*. The continuity of this campaign with the struggle for a proletarian party in our time is recorded in this volume, as well as in *Cuba and the Coming American Revolution* and the preface to the 2002 edition of *The History of American Trotskyism, 1928–38*.

Introduction

BY JACK BARNES

To this day I have a vivid memory of looking out at the 1,000 people gathered in the auditorium at the Illinois Institute of Technology in Chicago on New Year's Eve 1982–83. It was the second evening of a socialist educational conference held in conjunction with the twenty-second national convention of the Young Socialist Alliance. I had entitled a talk I had been asked to give "Their Trotsky and Ours," but the meeting that night was not about Leon Trotsky. It was about the members of the Socialist Workers Party, young socialists, co-workers, and party supporters—what they had accomplished, who they had become, in the midst of momentous world events they had responded to over the past half decade. It was about the coming American revolution.

Some four years earlier, at the beginning of 1978, the Socialist Workers Party had made a political turn to get the overwhelming majority of our cadres and leaders into the industrial working class and unions. We were shaking off residual forms of what Farrell Dobbs called the "semisectarian existence" imposed on us since the retreat of the working class at the end of the 1940s and the ensuing postwar expansion of finance capital. We had begun rebuilding organized units of party members in the industrial unions—nationwide trade union fractions. Communist political work in the labor movement was being carried out by women and men most of whom had been won to the revolutionary party over the previous two decades as young socialists actively engaged in battles for Black and Chicano rights, the anti-Vietnam War movement, the defense and distribution of the ideas of Malcolm X, struggles for women's liberation, and the defense of the Cuban Revolution. Above all, they were determined to emulate the intransigence and esprit de corps of those who made the Cuban Revolution. These were the people who formed the big majority of those present in the auditorium. They enjoyed proletarian politics; they looked forward to enjoying class combat.

The SWP and YSA were deeply involved at the time in getting out the truth about the advancing popular revolutions in Grenada and Nicaragua, and defending the workers and farmers governments in those countries against Washington's economic sabotage, CIA operations, and military aggression. Fewer than three years before, in 1979, these regimes had come to power through revolutionary struggles, and with those victories, prospects for extending the socialist revolution in the Americas—opened some two decades earlier with the triumph in Cuba—had been utterly transformed. The liberation struggle in El Salvador had gotten a powerful boost from the Nicaraguan victory. Half a world away, the "Peacock Throne" of the shah of Iran—U.S. imperialism's strongest bastion in the Arab/Persian Gulf—had also been toppled by a mass popular insurrection at the opening of 1979. The historic victory of the Vietnamese people over Washington's murderous war was still part of our common experience, and our fight to get the U.S. troops out was still fresh in our minds. Freedom forces in southern Africa, with the aid of a powerful contingent of volunteers from the Revolutionary Armed Forces of Cuba, were making new advances.

Socialist workers in the United States were deeply involved in the fights of working people against the employers' giveback demands. We were campaigning inside and outside the unions, and among workers, farmers, and youth, to mobilize solidarity with working people and their revolutionary battles in Central America and the Caribbean, and were taking co-workers to these countries to see for themselves. The *Militant* and *Perspectiva Mundial* had become the most reliable sources of accurate information on these revolutions, and the party was making special efforts to sell these periodicals on the job and in front of factory gates and mine portals. Pathfinder Press was expanding publication of writings and speeches by Fidel Castro and Ernesto Che Guevara, as well as the words of leaders of the workers and farmers government in Nicaragua and of Maurice Bishop in Grenada (and soon, with the Burkina Faso revolution in western Africa, the words of its outstanding leader Thomas Sankara).

The Socialist Workers Party was becoming more proletarian in composition—in daily life—as well as in program. The unfolding revolutions in Central America and the Caribbean were underlining for us once again how, with working-class leadership, the toilers can use a workers and farmers government to advance toward the expropriation of the exploiters and oppressors, the establishment of the dictatorship of the proletariat. As we lived through these revolutionary struggles day by day, we were becoming better equipped to draw clarity and strength from our communist political heritage. We could see and understand more richly and act with greater confidence on the continuity of our program and strategy, a program and strategy going back to the origins of the modern communist workers movement in 1847–48, when Karl Marx and Frederick Engels first shouldered leadership responsibilities in a revolutionary workers organization. We were hungry to better arm ourselves with the programmatic and strategic conquests of the Communist International, established sixty years earlier under the leadership of Lenin and the victorious Bolshevik party.

The SWP in 1980 had launched a leadership school where twice a year some dozen members of the National Committee leading the turn to industry took six months away from other party responsibilities to study the political writings of Marx and Engels—and, as a bonus, to study Spanish as well. Over the year prior to the Chicago meeting that New Year's Eve, each party branch had begun organizing schools in which every member, young socialist, and candidate for membership in the area participated in systematic study of the political works of Lenin, including the Comintern reports and resolutions that between 1919 and 1922 he and Leon Trotsky more than anyone else had shaped. In a sense, the night was a graduation exercise for all of us across every generation in the party who had together systematically worked our way through the first term in the Lenin schools.

These schools had helped us understand the twin foundations of Bolshevism: a communist, world program and a proletarian cadre. Following Lenin's death in early 1924, Leon Trotsky had led the fight in the world communist movement to continue the Bolshevik course in face of the assault on it by a growing, privileged bureaucratic caste in the Soviet Union.

"In our epoch, which is the epoch of imperialism, i.e., of *world* economy and *world* politics," Trotsky had written in his 1928 criticism of Stalin's increasingly nationalist and class-collaborationist course, "not a single communist party can establish its program by proceeding solely or mainly from conditions and tendencies of developments in its own country. . . . An international communist program is in no case the sum total of national programs or an amalgam of their common features. The international program must proceed directly from an analysis of the conditions and tendencies of world economy and of the world political system taken as a whole in all its connections and contradictions, that is, with the mutually antagonistic interdependence of its separate parts. In the present epoch, to a much larger extent than in the past, the national orientation of the proletariat must and can flow only from a world orientation and not vice versa."

"Their Trotsky and Ours" is a reaffirmation of that truth. And it was a registration of what the cadres of the Socialist Workers Party were accomplishing as our lives became more marked by involvement in struggles by working people in mines, mills, factories, and fields across the United States, and by our deepening collaboration and exchange of experiences and ideas with revolutionists elsewhere in the Americas and worldwide. At the same time, it was a salute to the veteran combatants in the party, those who had been won to communism during the labor battles and working-class social movements of the 1930s and had taught us to act, and live, as proletarian revolutionists.

A few months later, in the spring of 1983, Mary-Alice Waters and I drove with Farrell Dobbs, the party's national secretary from 1953 to 1972, down to King City, a small town in California's Salinas Valley, to get away from the pressures of daily responsibilities in order to work with him in putting the finishing touches on the second volume of the series of books he was in the midst of writing, *Revolutionary Continuity: Marxist Leadership in the U.S.* We also wanted to get his political suggestions for editing "Their Trotsky and Ours" for publication in the new magazine of Marxist politics and theory, *New International*. These were the last two major political projects Farrell was able to work on before his death in October of that year.

As we were out walking one evening, Farrell told us he wouldn't have been able to write that second volume of *Revolutionary Continuity* with anything approaching the same life and concreteness if he hadn't simultaneously been reading the Lenin selections that party branches around the country were using in their schools. Rereading Lenin was like a "refreshing shower," he said. That volume of *Revolutionary Continuity* tells the story of the birth of the communist movement in the United States during the first years of the Soviet workers and peasants republic and of the Communist International.

Farrell looked at the changes our movement was going through at the beginning of the 1980s in the same way as he did the historic events he was writing about, that is, from the standpoint of forging the leadership of communist workers parties competent to lead the toilers to victory. As he wrote in the preface to that second volume of *Revolutionary Continuity*, "the efforts by the Marxist wing of the workers' movement to gather the cadres of a proletarian revolutionary party needed to lead the fight to end capitalist rule, establish a workers and farmers government, and open the road to a socialist order" are decisive. Farrell dedicated the book "To the leadership of the Cuban Communist Party," "To the men and women of the New Jewel Movement of Grenada and the Sandinista National Liberation Front of Nicaragua," and "To the heroic combatants of the Farabundo Martí National Liberation Front" of El Salvador.

Another irreplaceable contribution to "Their Trotsky and Ours" was made by veteran party leader Joseph Hansen. Joe completed the introduction to his book *Dynamics of the Cuban Revolution* as we were generalizing the turn to industry in the spring of 1978. He died in January 1979, a few months before the victories in Grenada and Nicaragua. The contributions he had made for several decades, however, as part of the central leadership of the party and world communist movement—on the key programmatic question at the heart of "Their Trotsky and Ours," the nature of a workers and farmers government and its relation to the toilers' fight to overturn capitalist social relations and establish a workers state—provided the political tools we needed to understand and respond to those revolutions and join forces with them as communist partisans.

In the 1960s Joe had helped blaze a trail for the SWP leadership in understanding the political dynamics of the workers and farmers governments that came to power during post–World War II revolutions, especially in Yugoslavia, China, Algeria, and Cuba. He concluded that these transitional regimes are "the first form of government that can be expected to appear as the result of a successful anticapitalist revolution." This had been true of the initial Soviet government established under Bolshevik leadership in Russia in October 1917. Similar regimes had emerged after World War II with the revolutions in Yugoslavia and China, despite their Stalinist leaderships. (Because of the massive weight of the peasantry in the Chinese revolution, Joe considered it the biggest theoretical challenge of all, and it took him longer—to 1969—to be satisfied that its dynamics fit the workers and farmers government analysis.) The popular revo-

HALF PRICE BOOKS

EST. 1972

Half Price Books #126
1205 Johnson Ferry Rd, St. 106
Marietta, GA 30068

03-17-23 7:48 PM
Store #0126 / Cashier Alvarenga J / Reg 2
Sale # 237742

SALE TRANSACTION

Their Trotsky and Ours   351613556U
1 @5.99 $5.99

1 Item in Transaction

Subtotal $5.99
Sales Tax (6.0% on $5.99) $0.36
TOTAL $6.35

PAYMENT TYPE
VISA 2647 $6.35

Thanks for shopping at Half Price Books!

H020126002237742 2

HALF PRICE BOOKS

YOUR FAVORITE LOCAL BOOKSTORE. EVERYWHERE.

WHEN OUR STORES ARE CLOSED,
JUST OPEN YOUR BROWSER.
SHOP HPB.COM FOR MILLIONS
MORE TREASURES ONLINE.

JOIN THE HPB EMAIL LIST AT
HPB.COM/JOIN & GET A
10% OFF COUPON TO SAVE ON
YOUR NEXT PURCHASE IN STORE.

STORE RETURN POLICY

Cash refunds and charge card credits on all merchandise are
available within 7 days of purchase with receipt. Merchandise
charged to a credit card will be credited to your account.
Exchange or store credit only for returns made with a gift receipt
within 30 days of purchase date. Exchange or store credit will
be issued for merchandise returned within 30 days with receipt.
Cash refunds for purchases made by check are available after 12
business days, and are then subject to the time limitations stated
above. Please include original packaging and price tag when
making a return. Proper I.D. and phone number may be required
where permitted. We reserve the right to limit or decline refunds.

Gift cards cannot be returned for cash, except as required by law.

lutionary governments established in Cuba in 1959 under the leadership of the Rebel Army and July 26 Movement, and in Algeria in 1962 under the forces in the National Liberation Front led by Ahmed Ben Bella, confirmed the pattern.

All these governments, notwithstanding differences in the class structure and in the caliber of leadership in each country, did serve as "the first form of government . . . to appear as the result of a successful anticapitalist revolution." They were an antechamber to the dictatorship of the proletariat—that is, they provided a bridge to the overturn of capitalist social relations by the toilers and consolidation of a workers state, an instrument with which to advance that goal. But history also taught us, Joe stressed—and the case of Algeria demonstrated—that this outcome is not settled by the initial revolutionary victory itself. It is far from automatic, very far. The central communist leadership task in such a government is to mobilize and raise the political consciousness of an increasingly weighty fighting alliance of workers and farmers, responding to and leading the initiatives of the toilers as they deepen the inroads into the privileges and prerogatives of property in the hands of the landlords and capitalists.

In coming to these conclusions, which were incorporated in reports and resolutions adopted by the Socialist Workers Party, Joe kept reaching for the lessons of the fight for power, and the *exercise* of power, that had been drawn by the Communist International in Lenin's time. Neither Joe nor Farrell had been old enough to be politically active during the early years of the Russian Revolution. But each of them had been a young party member in the mid-1930s when our movement concluded, following Trotsky's initiative, that Hitler's uncontested rise to power demonstrated that it was no longer possible to reform the Stalin-led Comintern and instead turned our efforts to build a new revolutionary international. The German Communist Party had let the working class go down to defeat without a fight, refusing to campaign for a united front with the Social Democratic Party and the trade unions to take on the national socialists' goon squads in combat. On top of that, the Comintern and its parties were already so politically corrupted that there was no rebellion in their ranks against the disastrous course that led to the greatest defeat of the twentieth century.

Both Joe and Farrell had been trained by Trotsky to understand that the new world movement that had to be built needed no new program and strategy. Pull together the reports and resolutions hammered out in struggle by the Bolshevik leadership of the Comintern, under Lenin's political guidance, Trotsky told his secretariat in exile in 1933. *That's* our program.

James P. Cannon—a founding leader of the SWP who had been a pioneer of American communism and a delegate to congresses of the Communist International—opened his book *The History of American Trotskyism: 1928–38—Report of a Participant* with precisely that point: "We have no new revelation: Trotskyism is not a new movement, a new doctrine, but the restoration, the revival of genuine Marxism as it was expounded and practiced in the Russian Revolution and in the early days of the Communist International."

Our movement has not referred to itself as Trotskyist for many years. The reasons are explained in this book. But to this day we still have "no new revelation." In fact, less so than ever. Since the 1970s, as we have deepened our proletarianization, concretized our understanding of workers and farmers governments, and solidarized with the proletarian internationalist course of the leadership of the Cuban Revolution, we too have turned back to the political record and conquests of Bolshevism and the Communist International in Lenin's time. "Their Trotsky and Ours" is a product of that political course.

At the time the talk was given and first published, it was treated as a sensation, a virtual scandal, by the leaders of most of the organizations in the world that called themselves Trotskyists, a number of whom sent emissaries to the gathering with concealed tape recorders. The majority leadership of the Fourth International, with which the Socialist Workers Party was then fraternally associated, was among them. But in fact it was a tempest in a tea cup. None of those who voiced the greatest outrage were actually interested in the political and strategic questions addressed in these pages. They had long before turned away from the struggle for a proletarian party. They rejected the perspective of the fight for workers and farmers governments. None ever attempted to answer the arguments raised here. Over the next several years the programmatic positions and organizational methods of most of the groups in the Fourth International bore less and less connection to the Marxist and Bolshevik foundations on which our world movement had been launched a half century earlier—and on which the SWP and its sister communist leagues in a number of countries stood. Well before the end of the 1980s we had gone our separate ways—they, deeper into the centrist swamp of middle-class radical politics, and we, toward building proletarian parties and advancing the prospects of a new communist international.

As the turn to industry expanded the day-by-day life and work of SWP members with broader and more geographically diverse layers of working people across the United States, we also took a new look at the centrality of the worker-farmer alliance to revolutionary prospects in this country. In 1967 the party had dropped "farmers" from the "workers and farmers government" slogan. But the deepening involvement of party cadres in the 1970s and early 1980s in struggles of working people in town and country—our experiences, as unionists, with farmers—convinced us that this had been an error. We recognized that farmers would have substantial political weight in building any mass revolutionary movement in the United States, and that the class political alliance captured in the workers and farmers government slogan concretized a political course necessary for any victorious proletarian revolution here. At our 1984 convention, the SWP voted to amend Article II of the party constitution to read: "The purpose of the party shall be to educate and organize the working class in order to establish a workers and farmers government, which will abolish capitalism in the United States and join in the worldwide struggle for socialism."

＊

As this twentieth anniversary edition is being produced, together with new Spanish and French translations of it, "Their Trotsky and Ours" is one of the readings that is being studied and discussed in socialist summer schools organized in cities across the United States and internationally. Young socialists and others are participating alongside communist veterans of the turn to industry and party cadres from several generations. The purpose of the school, as explained in its syllabus, "is not just to read or reread a book or an article, but rather to approach these works through the lens of experiences the party and YS are living through today in the United States and internationally and the unfolding opportunities we can take advantage of."

It is those experiences and opportunities, in fact, that seemed to push us toward this new edition of "Their Trotsky and Ours."

When an imperialist power goes to war, all organizations that claim to speak for the interests of the working class are put to the test. Those without a communist program and proletarian composition are whipsawed by the patriotic pressures of bourgeois public opinion, either succumbing to them politically, or even beginning to shatter under the blows.

In early 1991 the U.S. government waged a brutal war against the people of Iraq, in which as many as two hundred thousand Iraqi civilians and soldiers were killed during six weeks of daily bombing and missile attacks and a one-hundred-hour invasion. The outcome of that murderous war was politically demoralizing to workers and farmers the world over, even more so to those in Iraq itself, since the Iraqi regime, following its indefensible invasion of Kuwait, organized virtually no resistance against Washington's final assault. The U.S. rulers did not succeed in imposing an imperialist protectorate in Iraq in order to compensate for the loss of the shah's regime in Iran twelve years earlier—their goal in the war—but at the same time they paid little price for their uncontested bloodletting.

Because of the roots the Socialist Workers Party and other

Communist Leagues had put down through the turn to the industrial working class and unions for more than a decade, the cadres of our organizations passed the test of the Gulf War, confidently moving more deeply into our class in the midst of the conflict to carry out a working-class campaign against imperialism and its war.

Since the closing years of the 1990s there has been a rise in resistance among vanguard workers and farmers in the United States. Other imperialist countries, with the exception still of Japan, have been marked by a similar shift. It took us a while to recognize the small beginnings of these changes, adjust to them, and start acting on the new opportunities. The pressing need to do so was the central question before a joint conference of the party and Young Socialists held in Los Angeles in December 1998. In the summary talk to that gathering on behalf of the SWP leadership, I pointed to the political importance for building our movement of these initially unconnected openings among vanguard working people in various industries and regions. That talk was published a few months later, under the title "A Sea Change in Working-Class Politics," as the opening chapter of the book *Capitalism's World Disorder*.

It had become clear, we emphasized, "that no matter what the legacy—in an industry, in a union, in a region, among any segment of working people—no matter how limited the results of previous struggles, what happens now in any struggle has less and less connection to earlier defeats. Using your peripheral vision to find the fighters in the working class and among its allies becomes more and more valuable. They are often there. It's like becoming a good point guard. Develop your peripheral vision. Teammates are there!"

In her 1999 preface to the Spanish translation of *The Changing Face of U.S. Politics*, which is the record of the party's turn to the industrial working class and unions from 1978 through the early 1990s, Mary-Alice Waters developed this point further. Together with "A Sea Change in Working-Class Politics," that preface was discussed in party branches and then adopted as a guide to action by the April 1999 SWP convention. The preface is now included in the new 2002 English edition of *The Changing Face of U.S. Politics,* and appears in a new 2002 edition of the French translation.

The vanguard currents and individuals we keep running into among layers of workers and farmers, Waters says,

> are meeting each other in the course of this resistance, hungry for solidarity and unity in struggle, hungry to march shoulder to shoulder, as together we strengthen and learn from each other's fights against the effects of wage slavery and debt slavery. Through the actions we are involved in, we learn to know and trust each other. We find ways to communicate, even if we don't yet know each other's languages well. We read and discuss explanations for and alternatives to the devastating future working people increasingly anticipate the capitalist system has in store for us all.

As we've followed these lines of resistance among working people in city and countryside, we've also displayed the courage of our convictions, adjusting the party's organizational forms to meet political needs. We've established new and smaller units of the party in areas of the country where we've become part of vanguard layers of coal miners, garment and textile workers, packinghouse workers, and others engaged in struggles. We've relocated bookstores so we can organize our political work out of workers districts in cities across the country. Where we've had branches for many years, we've used these trimmer units as models. All these steps are taking us more deeply into the union skirmishes and initial stirrings of social movements of our class and its allies that are harbingers of working-class resistance that will be mounted in face of increasingly violent capitalist assaults.

At the same time, young socialists have been meeting youth in the United States and other imperialist countries who are attracted to these proletarian struggles, as well as young people engaged in fights against imperialist oppression and exploitation from Haiti to the South Pacific islands of Kanaky (New Caledonia), from countries across the Middle East and Africa, to Venezuela and elsewhere in the Americas. The openings to win layers of these revolutionary-minded youth to communism have increased with the disintegration in the early 1990s of the world Stalinist movement, which for more than six decades, under the hijacked banner of Marxism, had organized from one continent to the next defeats of revolutions, assassinations of proletarian leaders, and demoralization and depoliticization of militants deeply immersed in struggles for national liberation and socialism.

These are the reasons, above all, why there is a need and a demand for a new edition of "Their Trotsky and Ours," which will also appear almost simultaneously in Spanish and French. These are the reasons it is being studied across the country at socialist summer schools, along with *The Changing Face of U.S. Politics* and James P. Cannon's *The History of American Trotskyism: 1928–38—Report of a Participant*, which is being produced simultaneously with this one in a new edition—and for the first time ever in Spanish and French.

*

The text and footnotes of "Their Trotsky and Ours" have been brought in line with subsequent and improved translations and printings of some of the quoted material. As it more and more becomes the norm for many Pathfinder titles to be published simultaneously in English, Spanish, and French—for use by workers doing political work in these languages—the collective effort on the translations helps clarify and politically sharpen elements of the original as well. Further editorial work has incorporated the fruits of these labors and eliminated unnecessary obstacles to reading and understanding "Their Trotsky and Ours" today.

From the translations, to the formatting and proofreading, to the final printing of the text and covers, the publication of books such as this one would not be possible without the efforts of hundreds of volunteers around the world who are members or organized supporters of the communist movement. Without the proletarianization of the party over the past quarter century, we could not have maintained and expanded a communist publishing program and printshop that enables us to get the invaluable lessons of 150 years of working-class struggle into the hands of vanguard fighters who recognize the need for broader political perspectives in order not only to fight successfully but also to win.

Nor would we have been able to build an auxiliary organization of supporters of the communist movement worldwide that has taken in hand the digital preparation, proofreading, graphics work, and other tasks that must be accomplished in order to keep revolutionary books and pamphlets in print and to produce new ones such as this in a timely way to meet pressing political needs and opportunities.

*

Much has happened in world politics since "Their Trotsky and Ours" was first published. The mold-shattering events of the last two decades have increased both the timeliness and political urgency of the fundamental points dealt with in these pages.

Neither the workers and farmers government in Grenada nor the one in Nicaragua went forward to the expropriation of the capitalists and landlords and establishment of a workers state. In October 1983 the workers and farmers government in Grenada was overthrown in a coup organized by a Stalinist faction in the governing New Jewel Movement. The revolution's central leader Maurice Bishop, along with dozens of other revolutionary leaders and Grenadian citizens, were murdered. By 1988 the leadership of the Sandinista National Liberation Front in Nicaragua had united around a course that sharply reversed the proletarian trajectory of the opening years of the revolution. With the defeat in Nicaragua, the revolutionary advances in nearby El Salvador eroded further and were soon reversed.

Our movement has produced, and actively campaigned to circulate, the record of the achievements of these revolutionary struggles and Marxist explanations of the lessons from their defeats. These materials can be found in the Pathfinder books *Maurice Bishop Speaks* and *Sandinistas Speak*, as well as in several issues of *New International* magazine: "The Second Assassination of Maurice Bishop" by Steve Clark; "The Rise and Fall of the Nicaraguan Revolution," a collection of reports and resolutions adopted by the Socialist Workers Party; and "U.S. Imperialism Has Lost the Cold War" by Jack Barnes.

Despite these blows in Central America and the Caribbean, and despite enormous political and economic pressures bearing down on the Cuban Revolution over the past twelve years, millions of working people and their leadership in Cuba continue to act as proletarian internationalists. Their courage, political consciousness, class solidarity, and implacable determination continue to set a revolutionary example for workers and farmers the world over, including here in the United States. "They are communists. And that is what we are, too"—that simple statement remains as true today as when it was asserted to young socialists and others in Chicago twenty years ago.

As this book goes to press early in the summer of 2002, the administration of President George W. Bush, with broad bipartisan backing, has announced plans to take "preemptive action" against those, at home and abroad, whom the U.S. rulers brand as "terrorists" or as linked to a worldwide "axis of evil." After hundreds of noncitizens have been held without charges in U.S. jails, many for nearly a year, Washington has now begun throwing U.S. citizens into military prisons as well. They are being denied even their most basic constitutional rights to know the charges against them, to legal counsel, or to the presumption of innocence. Washington is laying the political and military groundwork for "preemptive action" against Iraq and other governments and peoples the U.S. rulers consider strong enough to develop meaningful defenses against the assaults Washington is pressing.

History has shown that small revolutionary organizations will face not only the stern test of wars and repression, but also the potentially shattering opportunities that can emerge unexpectedly—and explosively—when strikes and social struggles erupt. As that happens, communist parties not only recruit many new members. They also fuse with other workers organizations moving in the same direction and grow into mass proletarian parties contesting to lead workers and farmers to power. This assumes that well beforehand their cadres have absorbed and grown comfortable with a world communist program and strategy, are proletarian in life and work, derive deep satisfaction from—have fun—doing politics, and have forged a leadership with an acute sense of what to do next. These cadres must already be functioning as part of a disciplined proletarian party, at one with those toilers being targeted by the employers and their state. Otherwise these organizations will be disoriented and broken in face of wrenching crises and enormous opportunities alike.

Farrell Dobbs, Joe Hansen, Jim Cannon, and other leaders of the Socialist Workers Party have all been firm believers in the fact that we'll never succeed in building a proletarian combat party in the United States if we start looking around for somebody other than the ranks of our own organization to hammer out concrete tactics and a political line on the class struggle. Or, conversely, if we start trying to dictate program and tactics to revolutionary-minded working people and youth in other countries. Joe explained this course of conduct in his 1975 talk, *James P. Cannon: The Internationalist*, an invaluable companion to "Their Trotsky and Ours."

Proletarian internationalism understood and carried out in that way—by integrating the cadres of the communist movement into the rising resistance of vanguard workers and farmers in the United States and the world over—is at the heart of "Their Trotsky and Ours." It is about building proletarian parties and a new world communist movement in which the political contributions of Marx, Engels, Lenin, Trotsky, and more contemporary revolutionary leaders can all be taken up and put to use by militants who come from different political origins and who judge each other not on the basis of preconception or prejudice but on the basis of deeds.

It is above all about getting ready every day with fellow militants for titanic class battles that lie ahead, and continuing to transform ourselves and our organizations as we do so.

JUNE 2002

The test of living revolutions

Ever since the first world imperialist slaughter led to the victory of the Russian workers and peasants under Bolshevik leadership in October 1917, the center of all politics has been the advance, defense, and consolidation of the socialist revolution against the imperialist system of exploitation, national oppression, and wars of aggression.

Central America and the Caribbean are today the front line in this ongoing battle between the exploiters and the toilers. That is where war is actually being waged—a counterrevolutionary war against the Sandinista-led workers and peasants government in Nicaragua; a civil war in El Salvador between the landlord-capitalist oligarchy and the forces of the workers and rural toilers led by the Farabundo Martí National Liberation Front; unrelenting military pressure, threats, and CIA operations against the Grenadian workers and farmers government and New Jewel Movement, and against revolutionary Cuba and its communist leadership. This is leading toward the regionalization of the war and the intensification of the class struggle throughout Central America.

Imperialism stands behind all the forces of tyranny and counterrevolution in the region. It provides massive amounts of military hardware and advisers. Washington directly utilizes increasing numbers of U.S. military forces as each successive escalation falls short of crushing the workers and peasants of Nicaragua and El Salvador, reversing the revolutionary course in Grenada, or dissuading Cuba from its unstinting solidarity with these struggles.

These wars between imperialism and imperialist-backed

forces on one side, and the oppressed and exploited on the other, are wars over the extension of the American socialist revolution opened by the triumph in Cuba twenty-four years ago. The stakes involve not only El Salvador, Nicaragua, and Grenada, but the fate of Cuba, as well. It's a package deal.

It is also in Central America and the Caribbean that the most important debates about revolutionary working-class strategy are going on today. This is important not only for revolutionary-minded workers elsewhere in the Caribbean and Latin America, but for those in North America and around the world who are building communist parties. What has happened since 1959 in Cuba, and since 1979 in Grenada and Nicaragua, is something that had not occurred since the 1917–23 period in Russia—victorious revolutions led by forces consciously committed to organizing and mobilizing the workers and poor farmers to overturn capitalist property relations, reorganize society along socialist lines, and aid others around the world seeking to throw off imperialist domination and exploitation.

The Cuban Communist Party, Sandinista National Liberation Front, New Jewel Movement, and Farabundo Martí National Liberation Front are reforging political links with the program and strategy adopted by the Communist International during its early years under a Russian Communist leadership that included Nikolai Bukharin, Karl Radek, Leon Trotsky, and Gregory Zinoviev, and was headed by Vladimir Lenin.

What has happened in this hemisphere over the past twenty-five years is not only the opening of the American socialist revolution, which would be important enough, but the reemergence of proletarian revolutionists in power—for the first time since the Stalinist-led bureaucracy put an end to such leadership in the Soviet Union and expunged proletarian internationalism from the Communist International more than a half century ago.

The leaders of the Cuban Communist Party have taken the political initiative in this process in their collaboration with revolutionists throughout the Americas. Along with their political and material support to revolutionary fighters, the Cuban leaders use many other means—writing articles, organizing conferences, making speeches—to advance their attempt to generalize lessons of revolutionary struggles.

The Socialist Workers Party, with its political heritage, and the organizations we are linked with on a world scale, can make an irreplaceable contribution to the political convergence of those working-class forces seeking to advance the revolutionary struggle against imperialism and for the socialist revolution. We bring our contribution not as a current that holds state power or even influences any major wing of the labor movement or of a national liberation struggle in any country today. We are communists who—in addition to the concepts from Marx, Engels, and Lenin that we hold in common with other revolutionists—also bring a rich appreciation of the efforts by members of the Russian Communist leadership around Lenin to maintain and apply an internationalist program and revolutionary proletarian strategy against the efforts to gut them by the developing bureaucratic caste led by Stalin. By the end of the 1920s, Trotsky alone among the central Bolshevik leaders was capable of carrying on that fight, and our movement is an organized political nucleus of workers that traces its roots to that struggle. That is *our* Trotsky.

In order to make this contribution, however, we have to clarify the relationship of our program to what is known in our movement as Trotsky's theory or strategy of permanent revolution.

Permanent revolution has actually been used by us in *three* ways since 1928.

In a broad sense, permanent revolution has served us as a synonym for revolutionary Marxism in our time. To us it has meant the continuity of genuine communist principles and strategy and opposition to the political course of the privileged bureaucratic caste that consolidated its power and privileges against the Soviet working class and poor peasantry. It has been the revolutionary alternative to the "second wave of Menshevism," to the abandonment of proletarian internationalism, by that caste and its followers in Stalinist parties around the world. It has signified the value and relevance of the lessons of the 1905 and 1917 revolutions in Russia, and opposition to political subordination of the fighting workers movement to the liberal bourgeoisie, popular frontism, and class collaborationism.

In this sense, there is nothing that sets permanent revolution apart from the general lessons from Marx, Engels, and Lenin on which all communists, including Trotsky, have based themselves. Nothing sets it apart from Marx's use of the term in 1850, nor from Lenin's use of "uninterrupted revolution" before the 1917 Russian Revolution. The use of permanent revolution in this sense serves only as a "trademark" to differentiate us from other revolutionists who share these ideas but not our terminology.

If this were the only meaning attributed to the term, it would have long ago been dropped as superfluous and open to misinterpretation. But more important questions are involved. In the rest of this article, therefore, this first meaning of permanent revolution will be set aside.

The second way that our movement has used the term permanent revolution is to refer to Trotsky's pre-1917 position on the class dynamics and strategy of the Russian Revolution, *as opposed to* that of the Bolshevik current. Our view has been that Trotsky was correct as against Lenin on these particular questions. In this respect, we followed Trotsky's own views in the post-1928 period.

Used in this second way, permanent revolution is wrong. Trotsky's pre-1917 views were revolutionary as opposed to those of the Mensheviks, who relied on the liberal bourgeoisie in Russia. But to the extent that Trotsky's strategy differed from Lenin's, it undervalued the workers' alliance with the peasantry as a whole—its poor, middle, and upper layers—in the struggle against tsarism and landlordism in Russia. It presented a less accurate view of how the class struggle would unfold, including how conflicts would develop among different layers of the peasantry as the working class took the leadership of the agricultural laborers and poor peasants to deepen the socialist course of the revolution. Thus, Trotsky had a less accurate understanding of the relationship between the democratic and socialist revolutions in Russia, and of the class forces and tasks of the proletariat in the transition from the democratic to the socialist tasks.

While there is not a one-to-one correspondence between overall strategy and concrete political positions, a strategic error left uncorrected over a period of time will generate wrong political positions. During some fifteen years of activity prior to 1917, Trotsky made important political errors on the agrarian program of the revolutionary proletariat, its approach to the fight against national oppression, and its policy in the struggle against imperialist war. Trotsky mistakenly viewed the political firmness and organizational discipline of the Bolsheviks as evidence of sectarianism, factionalism, and inflexibility, while he himself was conciliatory toward the Mensheviks and politically adapted to them at important junctures in the class struggle.

There is a third content that our movement has given to permanent revolution. Between 1928 and 1940, while Trotsky was still alive, and since then, we have used the term to describe the positions of our movement, especially in relation to the class struggle in the oppressed nations, that are uniquely based on and incorporate the strategic positions of Trotsky in the pre-1917 period as opposed to those of the Bolsheviks.

This use of permanent revolution poses the biggest *political* problem for us, because it has brought weaknesses into our movement associated with Trotsky's wrong pre-1917 theory. Above all, it has led to a tendency to concentrate solely on the proletariat's alliance with the agricultural laborers and poor peasants against the rural exploiters, undoubtedly a central task in the countryside, to the exclusion of recognizing the centrality of the proletariat's alliance with the broadest possible layers of the rural producers in the fight against imperialism and against the landlord-capitalist regimes in the colonial world. The world class struggle since World War II, including in this hemisphere since 1959, should convince us that to the extent those who are identified as Trotskyists act in accordance with these weaknesses in Trotsky's theory of permanent revolution, the door is opened to leftist biases and sectarian political errors.

Permanent revolution does not contribute today to arming either ourselves or other revolutionists to lead the working class and its allies to take power and use that power to advance the world socialist revolution. As a special or unique frame of reference it is an obstacle to reknitting our political continuity with Marx, Engels, Lenin, and the first four congresses of the Communist International. It has been an obstacle in our movement to an objective reading of the masters of Marxism, in particular the writings of Lenin.

If we are to learn what we can as part of the political convergence under way among proletarian revolutionists in the world today, and bring into that process Trotsky's enormous political contributions, then our movement must discard permanent revolution. If we don't, we will ultimately sacrifice the heart of Trotsky's political contribution—his fight during his last exile to build a revolutionary workers movement committed to continuing and developing genuine communism against the social democratic, Stalinist, and centrist distortions of it. Moreover, we will hinder our own progress toward a deeper integration into the organizations and struggles of the working class and its oppressed and exploited allies.

We need to view ourselves and our contributions in the way explained forty years ago by James P. Cannon, a founding leader of our movement in the United States. On the opening page of his *History of American Trotskyism, 1928–38*, Cannon stressed, "We have no new revelation: Trotskyism is not a new movement, a new doctrine, but the restoration, the revival of genuine Marxism as it was expounded and practiced in the Russian Revolution and in the early days of the Communist International."[1]

If we follow this advice from Cannon, then we can make

progress in reconquering our political continuity with Bolshevism and the Communist International under Lenin's leadership. That is the foundation on which we must build.

As we carry out that task, we will learn from other revolutionists who are striving to carry out communist principles of proletarian internationalism. What are these political lessons? The best place to start is the programmatic platform adopted by the Cuban Communist Party's First Congress in 1975.[2] Here is what it has to say:

> The Cuban Revolution—while presenting a whole series of specific features deriving from concrete national peculiarities and conditions and the international situation in which it is unfolding—has taken place in accordance with the fundamental laws of the historical process discovered by Marxism-Leninism, and has confirmed the main Leninist thesis on the revolution and the possibility of its uninterrupted course until turning into a socialist revolution.
>
> There is no insurmountable barrier between the democratic-popular and anti-imperialist stage and the socialist stage. In the era of imperialism, both are part of a single process, in which national-liberation and democratic measures—which at times have already a socialist tinge—pave the way for genuinely socialist ones. The decisive and defining element of this process is who leads it, which class wields political power.

The working-class strategy is to take, through its vanguard party, the leadership of the peasants and other oppressed and exploited allies. The initial stage of the revolution in Cuba, the platform says, "took the form of a democratic revolutionary dictatorship of the popular masses: of workers, peasants, the urban petty bourgeoisie and the other strata of the population, with interests opposed to imperialist and bourgeois-latifundist oligarchic domination.

"Now, in the second stage," that is, since late 1960, "that of socialist construction, it has taken the form of the dictatorship of the proletariat in alliance with the working peasants and all the other strata of our society with interests opposed to those of the capitalist regime."

The platform then goes into some detail about how this occurred in Cuba between 1959 and 1961. Key to the consolidation of the revolutionary victory, it explains, was that "the true power rested with the Rebel Army and the popular masses led by Fidel Castro; on his becoming Prime Minister, in February 1959, there followed a rapid elimination of the reactionary influence of the bourgeois elements that were part of the government."

The new government used its power to organize and mobilize the workers and peasants to begin an agrarian revolution, take action against imperialist domination of the country, upgrade conditions in the factories, create jobs, and implement a broad program of progressive measures in health care, literacy, education, democratic rights, and the elimination of discrimination against Black Cubans and against women. The platform explains:

> As a first step an anti-imperialist, agrarian, democratic and popular revolution was necessary to resolve the contradiction between the demands of the development of the productive forces and of the existing production relations. The national bourgeoisie was incapable of leading such a revolution because of its economic weakness, its subordination to Yankee imperialist interests and its fear of the action of the popular masses. This made it oppose even the measures of a national-liberation character of the first stage.

In Russia the Bolsheviks had rejected the Mensheviks' strategy of reliance on the bourgeoisie to lead the democratic revolution against tsarism and landlordism. The lessons from this and prior revolutionary experiences were incorporated into the program and strategy of the Communist International at its founding.

The Cuban CP platform goes on to explain the factors that

caused the Cuban capitalists to shrink from revolutionary action against landlordism and imperialist economic and political domination. It says:

> The interwoven economic interests of the Yankee monopolies, the bourgeois latifundist oligarchy and the rest of the national bourgeoisie would make any measure affecting any of these sections bring about immediate opposition and resistance of the bourgeoisie as a bloc. In conditions of economic and ideological domination by imperialism, measures that do not even go beyond the bourgeois democratic framework are generally rejected by the bourgeoisie of dependent countries. In these countries, the bourgeoisie fears that the development of the revolutionary process will inevitably lead to socialism.
>
> This situation, in which the objectives of national liberation and of a democratic nature had to be implemented by the working class at the head of the State power, conditioned the close interrelationship between the measures and tasks of the first and the second stages of our Revolution and the uninterrupted character of the transformations leading to the transition from one stage to the other in the context of a single revolutionary process.

Leaders of the Cuban CP presented these and related ideas recently at an International Conference on the Revolutionary Process in Latin America and the Caribbean, held in Havana in April 1982 under the auspices of the party's Central Committee. The conference was attended by representatives of thirty-five Latin American organizations, including both Communist parties and other groups. The participation of delegations of revolutionary leaders from Nicaragua, Grenada, El Salvador, and Guatemala was singled out for special mention at the opening of the conference.

I want to take note of one aspect, among many others, of the presentation there by Cuban CP Central Committee member Jesús Montané, which was dedicated to Che Guevara.[3] It follows directly from the above section of the Cuban CP platform.

"On this continent," Montané says, "we are witnessing an inseparable merger of the class and national struggles, a unique combination of the fight for democracy and for socialism, the fight for anti-imperialist liberation together with urban and rural workers' actions against capitalist exploitation." This combination, he says, will be reflected in the strategy and tactics of many parties and organizations on the left as they advance and gain new experiences.

The character of imperialist domination and its devastating impact on the workers and peasants of the Americas, Montané explains, "strengthen our conviction that this continent is about to give birth to a revolution that will lead to socialism and, as compañero Fidel Castro said recently, it will be as difficult to prevent as the labor of a pregnant whale."

Montané continued that in asserting this, Cuban Communists "aren't guilty of heedless optimism, nor do we ignore the difficulties we must overcome in carrying out a process that amounts to liquidating U.S. imperialism. We know that it will necessarily be a long, rough, complex process that will fill an entire historic epoch."

And, we might add, if the end result is the liquidation of U.S. imperialism, working people in the United States will be deeply involved, as well—for an extended period.

Montané points out that recognizing the necessarily socialist outcome of these revolutions in the Americas does not answer the question of the immediate and transitional demands around which the struggle for power will be fought, which are first of all those of the democratic and anti-imperialist struggle. "The processes of national liberation and the construction of socialism in this area will not be governed by rigid patterns or standards," he says. Each revolutionary party will have to chart a course based on its own experiences and the concrete conditions and class relations in each country.

Another speech at the same conference was given by Manuel Piñeiro, also a Central Committee member of the Cuban

Communist Party.[4] This speech is entitled, "Unity, the Masses, and Arms in the Struggle for Power"—what Piñeiro, citing Fidel Castro, calls "the three ingredients decisive to successfully reaching the revolutionary triumph."

Comrade Piñeiro, takes a critical look at some of the lessons the Cubans have learned over two decades about these three aspects of the strategy for revolution.

He explains the need for two kinds of unity. One is what we would call an anti-imperialist united front of the forces willing to fight against the oligarchy, dictatorial rule, and imperialist oppression. Such unity is very important, he says, "on the condition that the revolutionary parties and organizations succeed in consolidating the leadership nucleus in such fronts."

This points to the need for another kind of unity—unity of the revolutionists. This can't be based on "artificial steps that later turn out to be counterproductive," Piñeiro says. Instead, "It is common knowledge that the best form of advancing unity is through collaboration in concrete struggles." Such unity will advance the proletariat toward taking the leadership of all its allies in making the revolution. "The proletarian revolution in Latin America is at the same time a people's revolution," he explains.

Piñeiro's theme on the masses is very simple. It is not possible to take power in the name of the masses; the masses must be led to take power themselves. "The incorporation of the masses into the revolution," he says, "is the sole motor force capable of guaranteeing" both the conquest of power and its preservation.

This basic precept of revolutionary strategy explained by Piñeiro was developed in detail at the Third Congress of the Communist International in 1921.[5] At that congress, Lenin led a fight against ultralefts to incorporate into the resolution on tactics the need for communists not only to win a majority of the proletariat, but also a mass following among the exploited allies of the proletariat, above all the rural toilers.

In this regard, Piñeiro continues, two opposite errors can be made: first, "substituting the vanguard for the . . . masses," leading to premature confrontations and missing more opportune moments; or second, "postponing certain actions again and again, using the subterfuge that the masses are not adequately prepared to move toward the conquest of power."

Piñeiro also deals with the use of demands by revolutionists—immediate and democratic demands, and their relation to demands that point toward the revolutionary transition to a new government of the workers and peasants to struggle against the bourgeoisie. Revolutionists can learn a great deal by studying the experiences in Cuba, Nicaragua, and Grenada, he says. But "there are no recipes or general formulas" for how to educate, mobilize, and organize the masses for the conquest of power.

The same is true for the third "decisive ingredient"—arming the workers and peasants. Here too, Piñeiro says, there is no "single continental strategy." The tasks of revolutionists vary depending on concrete conditions—whether they are operating under rightist dictatorships or in a situation where greater democratic rights exist, for example.

Piñeiro warns that "false dichotomies have been put forward that counterpose armed and nonarmed forms of struggle.

"In our opinion," he says, "the revolutionary content of any form of struggle is measured by its results, that is, by the advance or retreat it implies for the final objectives of the popular masses."

Piñeiro stresses the danger of any "division between the political and military functions" in the party. Such a division, he says, "gives rise to a mutilation of both."

As organizations and individuals from various currents in the workers movement in the Caribbean and Latin America have gone through experiences in the fight against imperialism and landlord-capitalist oligarchies, they have been attracted to the Cuban Revolution and influenced by its leaders. This has been true of the Sandinista National Liberation Front in Nicaragua from its origins. Leaders of Grenada's New Jewel Movement have explained their political evolution from a current in the

Caribbean Black Power movement in the late 1960s and early 1970s to a revolutionary proletarian party, once again greatly aided by the example of the Cuban leadership and its views.

The revolutionists of the Salvadoran FMLN and its various components have also been shaped by the struggles and political discussions opened by the victory of the Cuban Revolution. I want to focus on one example: an article entitled, "Power, the Character and Path of the Revolution and the Unity of the Left," by Schafik Jorge Handal, who is an FMLN leader and general secretary of the Communist Party of El Salvador. This article has recently been reprinted in *Intercontinental Press*, making it easily available.[6]

Handal cites lessons from El Salvador, from the victories in Cuba and Nicaragua, and from the defeat in Chile as the source of his own changing views. He points out that "two great true revolutions have taken place" in Latin America—in Cuba and Nicaragua (he is excluding the English-speaking Caribbean for the purposes of this article). "In neither of these two cases was the Communist Party at the head," he says.

Why? This is a question, Handal explains, that all serious leaders and cadres of Communist parties have to answer. Otherwise they will never find ways of becoming part of the Marxist vanguard of coming revolutions. Handal then outlines the views he has come to on this question, and he seeks discussion from other revolutionists, too.

"The ABCs of Marxism-Leninism," Handal says, "teach us that the fundamental question of the revolution is the question of power"—taking political power and holding it. Handal is now convinced that his party and other CPs in Latin America have been guilty of acting contrary to these ABCs. They have acted on the basis of an "incorrect characterization of certain social processes and reformist policies in Latin America as 'revolutions.'" The Communist parties in these countries incorrectly cast themselves "in the role of just being a supportive force."

Handal recalls the example of Chile. Defeat there was not inevitable, he says. The problem was that Communists and others did not have "a solid orientation to really trying to resolve the problem of state power or to defend Allende's government" against escalating attacks from the capitalist class and its officer corps. No political organization had prepared the workers and peasants in Chile to take power.

Handal has come to the conclusion that while the social and economic program of revolutionists is important, it can come to naught without a strategy to lead the workers in organizing the popular masses—first and foremost the peasantry—in order to take power from the landlord-capitalist oligarchy and all its supporters. In this regard, he says that Lenin's April 1917 theses and other communist teachings during Lenin's lifetime "are still the models of how to judge the problem of power."

While the Latin American CPs established in the 1920s and 1930s, "stopped having the struggle for power central to their activity," Handal says, some new communist parties are now being built on firmer revolutionary foundations. In Cuba, where a Communist Party was forged in the first years after the revolution. In Nicaragua today. And, he is convinced this will happen in El Salvador, through an eventual fusion of the revolutionary proletarian forces there.

Handal explains that for almost two decades he and many other Communists in Latin America were convinced that the Cuban Revolution had been a "peculiar exception." In light of experiences in Nicaragua and El Salvador since 1979, he has now come to the opposite conclusion.

The Cuban Revolution, he says, demonstrated "a regular feature of the revolution in Latin America"—that "the revolution that matures here is the socialist revolution."

This does not mean that the revolutionary struggle for anti-imperialist demands, agrarian reform, and democracy is not on the agenda in Latin America, Handal stresses. Whereas he had previously believed that these democratic tasks were walled off from tasks of a socialist character, Cuba had shown the interrelationship between them. "What mobilizes the great masses to revolutionary action are the democratic and anti-imperialist slogans," Handal explains. And "the democratic anti-imperialist revolution can't be completed, nor can its gains be defended, without going on to socialism."

Handal then puts it another way: "One can't go to socialism except by the democratic anti-imperialist path, but neither can the democratic anti-imperialist revolution be consummated without going on to socialism.

"To the extent that between these two there is an essential and indissoluble connection," Handal explains, "they are facets of one revolution and not two revolutions." Rejecting this generalization, which was a fundamental part of the program of the Comintern under Lenin, the Salvadoran and most other Latin American CPs had "worked for decades with the idea of two revolutions."

As a result, Handal explains, the CP in El Salvador and other countries lost sight of the leading role of the working class in the revolution. "We convinced ourselves that the democratic revolution is not necessarily to be organized and promoted principally by us, but that we could limit ourselves to supporting it, and conform to this support role, in order to assure the range and breadth of the participating democratic forces."

The Nicaraguan Revolution led Handal to take a fresh look at the Cuban Revolution, and he is now convinced "that in the Latin American communist movement there has to be a tremendous ideological struggle to free ourselves from all that reformist ballast."

The Cuban Revolution demonstrated the necessity of building a leadership deeply involved in the mass struggles, organizing the workers and peasants, and at the same time recognizing that there is no peaceful road to power, and no road to power that relies upon any wing of the bourgeoisie. Only the working people, organized by a revolutionary party that provides both political and military leadership, can conquer power and use it to advance their own class interests. If sectors of the bourgeoisie will come part of the way along that road, then revolutionists can make use of such divisions to advance toward bringing down the old regime and establishing and consolidating a workers and farmers government.

For communists, Handal says, political work in mass struggles and organizations must have as its conscious aim the preparation of the workers and peasants to overthrow the dictatorship of capital and establish their own dictatorship. Unless *this* perspective is consciously thought out and advanced in practice, all the energetic mass work in the world will not result in a revolutionary victory.

Any idea that the workers can take power "bit by bit" is false, Handal says. "Rather, it will be indispensable, one way or another, to dismantle the state machinery of the capitalists and their imperialist masters, to erect a new State and a new Power.

"In such conditions it becomes evident that the peaceful route is not the path of revolution."

Of course, Handal says, the workers and peasants who are the great majority of society would prefer to take power peacefully. But the experience of the toilers in Latin America and worldwide has shown that the tiny handful of exploiters use massive violence to preserve their power, profits, and privileges—their class dictatorship. Therefore, revolutionists must recognize that historical fact and prepare the masses for it.

The workers, led by a revolutionary workers party, must organize their toiling allies to carry through the democratic, anti-imperialist revolution against the oligarchy—the landlords and capitalists. In the process of leading the toilers to victory, the working class and its communist vanguard will begin—depending upon the concrete material conditions and the relationship of class forces at home and abroad—to carry out the tasks of the socialist revolution, culminating in the expropriation of the capitalists and the reorganization of society on the basis of state property and economic planning.

These conclusions drawn by Handal are the lessons of Cuba, of Nicaragua, of the victories and of the defeats in Latin America. And these are the lessons we find when we go back to Lenin and to the program and strategy of the Bolshevik Party and the early Communist International.

It is not enough, however, to recognize the need for armed struggle, Handal continues. Communists must take every opportunity, under difficult underground conditions and in periods when there are legal or semilegal openings, to organize and mobilize the workers and peasants.

What was wrong with the Salvadoran CP's past activity, Handal explains, is not that it carried out electoral work. This "was right on the mark," he says. What wasn't "right on the mark" was the class-collaborationist political line and strategy of that electoral activity, which "engendered reformist ideas and illusions" among the leaders, cadres, and supporters of the CP.

Handal says that when the Salvadoran CP decided to reverse its previous course and join the military struggle against the dictatorship, it was not adequately prepared to put this decision into practice. The party already had a Military Commission, but this turned out to be an obstacle, not an aid. The commission was separated from the party and its leadership, Handal explains, whereas mastering the art of insurrection and the fundamentals of military strategy must be integrated into the party's overall political preparation to lead the toilers to take power.

To confront this obstacle to charting a revolutionary course, the Salvadoran CP held a congress in April 1979 and "abandoned the idea that the Military Commission was responsible for forming a military apparatus separate from the main body of the Party." The fault had not been with members of the commission, Handal stresses, but with the misconceptions and mistraining from the party's previous orientation. The problem had been "the inability of the Party as a body to organize and direct the armed struggle when the moment to do so arrives.

"This problem could only be resolved by converting the Party as a whole into both director and actor, not only in the political struggle, but in the armed struggle as well," Handal says, "making it the great combiner and director of all forms of struggle." The leading committees and their members began to "study the problems of the revolutionary armed struggle and train in military art and technique, not to dedicate all of them to the military apparatus, but to put into practice the conviction that the armed struggle of the Party should be organized, carried out and directed by the Party, its leadership bodies and its base."

This question was referred to in a general way in the speech by Cuban CP leader Manuel Piñeiro cited earlier. Most recent discussion of this particular aspect of revolutionary strategy has been limited to experiences since 1945 in China, Vietnam, and Cuba. But as we are discovering with the big majority of fundamental political and strategic questions, this too was taken up by the Communist International during Lenin's time. Here is what the resolution on "The Organizational Structure of Communist Parties" adopted at the third Comintern congress in 1921 had to say on the subject:

> Both the legal and illegal Communist Parties often understand illegal Communist organizational work to be the creation and maintenance of a closely knit and exclusively military organization, isolated from other aspects of Party work and organization. This is undoubtedly a mistaken view. In the pre-revolutionary period our military organization must be built primarily by general Communist Party work. The Party *as a whole* must become a *military organization* fighting for revolution. When isolated revolutionary military organizations are set up prematurely, they tend to become demoralized and break up because there is no directly useful Party work for them to do.[7]

Finally, Handal takes up another question in the specific Salvadoran context that Cuban leader Piñeiro deals with in a more general way—the question of unity among revolutionary forces committed in practice to the struggle against the dictatorship of the landlord-capitalist oligarchies in the Americas.

Handal is convinced that this type of unity is crucial to victory in El Salvador. The Communist parties in Latin America have for decades spurned cooperation with other revolutionary forces, he says, but this must change. It is the only way to build parties that are communist in action as well as name. That is what happened in Cuba. That is what is happening in Nicaragua. And that is what Handal advocates in El Salvador.

The process of unifying the revolutionary forces will not lead to automatic agreement on everything, he says. But "we debate while pronouncing ourselves in favor of the unity of the left."

The Salvadoran CP, Handal concludes, "is not the only detachment of the Latin American Communist Movement" that is debating this fundamental revolutionary change. He clearly expects quite a discussion on the perspectives he has laid out, including in his own party.

You don't have to agree with everything that Handal says in this article to recognize that it deserves serious attention. He raises questions being considered by a broad range of proletarian revolutionists attempting to find the road to do exactly what we want to do not only in Latin America and the Caribbean, but in North America as well—build communist parties that will lead the workers and their allies to defeat the capitalist ruling class and take power.

This is the central task that revolutionists have set themselves since the founding document drafted by Marx and Engels at the beginning of 1848 for the first proletarian communist organization, the Communist League. That document, which has come to be known as the Communist Manifesto, explained that the first task of the working class "is to raise the proletariat to the position of ruling class." The proletariat will then "use its political supremacy to wrest, by degrees, all capital from the bourgeoisie, to centralize all instruments of production in the hands of the State, *i.e.*, of the proletariat organised as the ruling class; and to increase the total of productive forces as rapidly as possible."[8]

In 1872 Marx and Engels wrote an introduction to a reissue of the Communist Manifesto. They noted that a bit more needed to be said now based on the experience of the working class, first, in the revolutions of 1848, and then verified by the Paris Commune of 1871, "where the proletariat for the first time held political power."

"One thing especially was proved by the Commune," Marx and Engels wrote, "the working class cannot simply lay hold of the ready-made State machinery, and wield it for its own purposes."[9] The proletariat has to smash the state apparatus of the old ruling classes and replace it with one of their own.

Nearly half a century later, the opening section of the platform of the Communist International, adopted at its First Congress in 1919, was entitled, "The Conquest of Political Power." It explained: "The key to victory for the proletariat lies in organizing its power and disorganizing that of the enemy; it entails smashing the bourgeois state apparatus while constructing a proletarian one."[10]

Basing itself squarely on these programmatic foundations laid by Marx, Engels, and the Comintern under Lenin, the 1938 founding document of the Fourth International, the Transitional Program, drafted by Leon Trotsky, affirmed:

"The chief accusation which the Fourth International advances against the traditional organizations of the proletariat is the fact that they do not wish to tear themselves away from the political semicorpse of the bourgeoisie." In contrast, we say: "Break with the bourgeoisie, take the power!"

It went on: "The sections of the Fourth International should critically orient themselves at each new stage and advance such slogans as will aid the striving of the workers for independent politics, deepen the class character of these politics, destroy reformist and pacifist illusions, strengthen the connection of the vanguard with the masses, and prepare the revolutionary conquest of power."[11]

Lead the toilers toward the revolutionary conquest of power, not to subordination to the needs or promises of the liberal bourgeoisie. That's our message, that's the spirit in which we build our party. This perspective—one that the Communist International was founded to advance and that our world movement seeks to continue—is the perspective put forward by the 1975 platform of the Cuban Communist Party, and in the speeches and articles by Comrades Montané, Piñeiro, and Handal.

These fundamental lessons have been confirmed by more than a century of working-class struggle, of revolutions that succeeded and those that were crushed. Each revolution has particular characteristics that are vital to understand, but there are also general lessons such as these. As Piñeiro puts it, "Every real social revolution is always also a daughter of the universal laws discovered by Marx, Engels, and Lenin."

These are the political principles and broad revolutionary strategy needed by the working class in all countries. Any attempt to somehow get around them will result in bloody defeat followed by deep demoralization. As our class goes through experiences, we draw lessons, generalize them, and apply and enrich them through further experiences in the class struggle. That is what a communist party does.

The questions addressed by Montané, Piñeiro, and Handal are the correct ones for anyone who wants to be a communist in Latin America today. They are relevant questions for communists in North America, too, and throughout the world. Not only because we, as internationalists, recognize that U.S. and Canadian workers have a big stake in the revolutions in the nations oppressed by imperialism, but also because of the weight of the Black and Chicano national questions in the United States and of the Quebecois national question in Canada.

The programmatic and strategic answers presented by the Central American and Caribbean leaders on the combined democratic and socialist character of the revolutions in Latin America, and the need for proletarian leadership of these revolutions, are communist ones. If there can be any doubt about that after reading the views of Montané, Piñeiro, and Handal, then take the time to study the 1970 article by Cuban vice president and CP Political Bureau member Carlos Rafael Rodríguez entitled "Lenin and the Colonial Question."[12] It anchors a view of revolutionary strategy for the oppressed nations in the fundamental programmatic positions hammered out by Marx and Engels and developed further, after the rise of imperialism, by the Bolshevik Party and Communist International under Lenin's leadership.

Rodríguez's article is a contribution to the strategic political questions that revolutionists are discussing and reconquering, based on their experiences in the class struggle.

There is no special "Castroist" revolutionary outlook or political current in the world today. That is a myth we should bury for good. The Cuban, Nicaraguan, Grenadian, and Salvadoran revolutionists have each made political contributions based on their particular experiences and the traditions of revolutionary struggle in their own countries. But what they are learning, enriching, and applying is the program of Marxism, not "Castroism." They are communists. And that is what we are, too.

As communists in the United States, we must do more than engage in solidarity work with these revolutions in Central America and the Caribbean, as essential as that is both for the workers there and in this country. If we are serious about building a revolutionary workers party in the United States, we must also listen to and learn from these comrades, who have put everything on the line for the defense and extension of the socialist revolution in Central America and the Caribbean. We must use their example to inspire revolutionary-minded workers in the United States and convince them that it is possible to establish a workers and farmers government.

We are living through one of the great turning points in modern world history. Socialist revolutions have been born and are being born in our hemisphere. And with them have emerged— for the first time since the Stalinist degeneration of the Communist International half a century ago—new, proletarian leaderships that head governments as well as mass parties.

The perspective opened up by the revolutionary leaderships in Central America and the Caribbean for a fusion of the forces struggling to build communist parties points the way forward *politically* toward a new international working-class movement—the goal of conscious proletarian revolutionists since 1848. That mass world revolutionary organization doesn't yet exist, and it's not right around the corner. But that is the direction the fighting revolutionary vanguard of our class is marching. And that is why the stakes are so high for us in learning from and contributing to the process of political discussion and clarification that, at whatever pace, can lay the groundwork for a new, mass, communist International.

Marxism, Bolshevism, and the Communist International

Our revolutionary political continuity, that of the modern working class, does not go back very far—only 135 years. It goes back to the generalizations adopted by the Communist League and presented in initial form in its manifesto, which Marx and Engels were assigned to draft, and in its organizational rules, which they also had a major role in preparing.

The lessons drawn by the leaders of the Cuban, Nicaraguan, Salvadoran, and Grenadian revolutions are part of this common revolutionary continuity. But determining just what, concretely, that consists of is a little more complicated than it might seem. Because political continuity is not like the doctrine of a church, which is ultimately judged right or wrong by some body of people who claim a direct line to someone or something you can't argue with. That is how the articles of a faith are settled.

But as Engels wrote just two months before the formation of the Communist League at the end of 1847, "Communism is not a doctrine but a *movement*; it proceeds not from principles but from *facts*. . . . Communism, insofar as it is a theory, is the theoretical expression of the position of the proletariat in this [class] struggle and the theoretical summation of the conditions for the liberation of the proletariat."[13]

Communists don't have any articles of faith. What we have, as Engels explained, is simply the political generalizations and strategic lessons from the experiences of a class that has been marching toward taking power ever since it was born and began to wage battles in its own name—*the modern working class.*

This needs to be thought about, because it is alien to the way people are taught to think by the schools and other institutions under capitalism. We are trained to think in terms of ideas and individuals that float above classes and material conditions. It is easy to slip into thinking that a political program has a life of its own, like the doctrine and rituals of a church or the masonic lodge.

These doctrines don't change until the body of people who determine them decide they should change. But that is not true of the proletariat's program, which is changed through clarification and enrichment with every major new experience in the class struggle.

Marx and Engels explained this materialist approach in the Communist Manifesto. Communists, the Manifesto explained, "do not set up any sectarian principles of their own, by which to shape and mold the proletarian movement." They "have no interests separate and apart from those of the proletariat as a whole."

What, then, does distinguish communist workers from the rest of their class? On the plane of practical action, Marx and Engels say, the communists are "the most advanced and resolute section" of the working class. On the plane of program and ideas, they have "the advantage of clearly understanding the line of march, the conditions, and the ultimate general results of the proletarian movement."[14]

Writing four years later to a founding member of the Communist League, then working to build the communist movement in North America, Marx explained that his own contribution to the theory of the revolutionary workers movement was not the discovery of the existence of classes or the class struggle, which many others had described and commented on. His own new contribution, Marx said, was to demonstrate "that class struggle necessarily leads to the *dictatorship of the proletariat.*"[15]

It is only by generalizing and drawing the lessons of the actual experiences of the working class that revolutionists develop a program and strategy that can help us lead our class toward that goal—the dictatorship of the proletariat. That is where our political continuity comes from.

Lenin said that without revolutionary theory, there can be no revolutionary movement. You hear that quotation so many times that it can sometimes lose its meaning. But it is important to think about what Lenin actually said. He didn't say that without revolutionary theory there can be no revolutionary *action*. That would be wrong. Horribly and disarmingly so. There can be, have been, and will continue to be revolutionary struggles by working people that are not guided by organizations equipped with revolutionary theory. Revolutionary struggles, but not a revolutionary *movement*. Because building a revolutionary movement, as opposed to action alone, necessitates a conscious generalization of lessons that our class has learned through struggle into a program and strategy, a political continuity, upon which revolutionary *organization* is based.

These lessons—what to do, and in some ways even more importantly, what not to do—have been paid for in blood many times over by our class. They are irreplaceable.

The fact that our program and strategy are rooted in the experience of the working class, however, also means that new experiences *change*, better enrich, our revolutionary continuity. They cannot alter past events, of course. But our political continuity is not frozen. It is the evolving consciousness of the vanguard of a class, expressed in program and strategy and embodied in revolutionary organizations and their cadres.

We incorporate new lessons while preserving old ones and understanding them in new ways. Our revolutionary continuity is a living thing. It is our *current* understanding of the rich lessons of revolutions and class battles that came before us, and this understanding changes as our class goes through new experiences.

The program of the Communist International was not only in continuity with but also far richer and more extensive than the program of the pre–World War I Bolshevik Party, for example. The world proletariat had gone through the first imperialist world war, the collapse of the Second International as a revolutionary organization, and the 1917 Russian Revolution.

These events, culminating in the establishment of the world's first workers state, had put all wings of the workers movement to the test. The Third International didn't just preserve what was best from the program of its forerunners, what had stood the test of titanic events. It also made additions and altered the weight and emphasis it gave to various aspects of this program.

Similarly, the Cuban Revolution, the extension of the socialist revolution by the Nicaraguan and Grenadian toilers, and the current battle in El Salvador—these experiences enrich and change the way we understand and apply our revolutionary continuity today. If new socialist revolutions didn't affect us this way, we would be finished as a revolutionary organization.

Questions that couldn't be answered definitively twenty-five years ago have been settled by the class struggle. For example, were all revolutions going to be led—and warped—by parties trained in the school of Stalinism? That could have seemed to be the case during the period between World War II and late 1959. We were confident that the answer was "no," but it was none-theless an open question until it was settled in *practice* by the victory of the Cuban Revolution.

I stress this question of continuity and change, because we are conservative, and correctly so, when it comes to program-matic changes. Trotsky warned: Think twice before you trim Marx's beard, comrades. The lessons of our class have been won at great cost, and are not something to be tinkered with light-mindedly. In fact, that serious attitude toward program is one thing that distinguishes proletarian revolutionists from petty-bourgeois dilettantes.

But each generation of working-class fighters must see these lessons through its own eyes, from the standpoint of the con-crete experiences it has gone through and anticipates. In that way, each generation understands its continuity more deeply, enriches it, uses those aspects that most directly relate to its own experiences, sees the point from this or that new angle given the particular problems it faces.

By stressing that our political continuity is a working-class continuity, one that only stretches back to the program of the first modern, scientific communist organization, I don't mean to say that we don't absorb lessons and draw inspiration from fighters in history who are not a direct part of this political, programmatic continuity.

One of the speeches I referred to earlier, for example, ends with a quotation from Fidel Castro naming an entire layer of fighters for the national liberation of Cuba before the working class came onto the scene as the leading force in that struggle—revolutionary figures such as José Martí and Antonio Maceo.

Or take the statement of purpose in the Young Socialist Alliance constitution. While explaining that the YSA is a Marxist organization, basing itself on the workers' struggle for political power, it also explains that the YSA draws inspiration from fighters against oppression in other historical periods, such as Sam Adams and Sojourner Truth and Susan B. Anthony, as well as revolutionary giants of our own era, such as Malcolm X, who was not yet a Marxist when his life and political evolution were brutally cut short by agents of the U.S. ruling class. However, our *political,* our *programmatic* continuity is more specific.

Events of the past twenty-five years have time and again taken us back to one particular period in that continuity, the discussions and documents of the Communist International (the Comintern). They have taken us back to the early years of the Communist International, when Lenin was alive, and leaders of the Russian Communist Party were trying to pass on lessons of the programmatic legacy of Marx and Engels, of the Russian Revolution, and of the world struggle it inspired. That revolution for the first time had achieved "the ultimate general results" forseen by the Communist Manifesto—the consolidation of the dictatorship of the proletariat.

Why have our experiences since 1959, and again since 1979, taken us back not only to the political writings of Marx and Engels, but also to the reports and resolutions of the Comintern? The reason is that the Cuban Revolution is a socialist revolution, led by a revolutionary leadership committed to deepening and extending that revolution, building a communist party to do this, and doing whatever is necessary to advance this revolutionary process. This is what the Communist International was established to do on a world scale. That's why the lessons from this historical period ring so true today.

Today we are able to study and understand the lessons from the Comintern in ways we couldn't in years past. We will learn more from studying the Comintern documents in the light of these experiences.

It's not that the program of the first five years of the Comintern has changed. *We've* changed, as the revolutionary class struggle has unfolded. We have become more proletarian—more working-class in the composition of our leadership and membership, not just our programmatic outlook. Our eyes are more open and our minds are more attuned. Things we have seen happen, forces we've seen come forward, fellow revolutionists that challenge us to advance our thinking—all this makes us better able to understand and apply the Comintern program to, and within, a living reality.

It's mind-boggling to take in not only what but how much the Communist International accomplished in its first five years.

The Bolshevik leaders assigned to the Executive Committee of the Communist International were Lenin, Bukharin, Radek, Trotsky, and Zinoviev. Under their leadership the Comintern laid the programmatic and strategic groundwork for revolutionary struggle for the dictatorship of the proletariat, including the slogan of the workers and farmers government; the fight by communist workers to transform the unions into revolutionary instruments of class struggle; the tactic of the united front; the place of the fight for workers' control in the line of march of the working class to power; the championing of the struggle for the emancipation of women; the proletariat's stance in the fight against imperialist domination and national oppression, including Black liberation in the United States; the roots of fascism and how to combat it; the organization and structure of Communist parties.

What I want to focus on here is the Comintern's integrated view of the world revolution. The Comintern for the first time incorporated two new elements decisive to the revolutionary struggle for workers and farmers governments and the dictatorship of the proletariat in the twentieth century.

First, the victory and consolidation of the Russian Soviet republic fundamentally changed the relationship of class forces in world politics. The Comintern recognized that mobilizing the international working class and its allies to defend this historic revolutionary conquest against imperialism was an integral part of extending the socialist revolution worldwide. "The struggle for Soviet Russia has become merged with the struggle against world capitalism," the manifesto of the second Comintern congress explained in 1920. "The question of Soviet Russia has become the touchstone by which all the organizations of the working class are tested."[16]

That is more true than ever today, when this initial conquest of the world working class has been augmented by the establishment of workers states in China, Korea, Vietnam, Eastern Europe, and Cuba, with more on the way in the Caribbean and Central America.

Second, the Comintern projected a course toward a truly *world* socialist revolution for the first time. Before then, the Marxist workers movement had considered socialist revolution to be a realistic perspective only in a relatively small number of industrialized countries, primarily in western Europe and North America. In large part, this had been an accurate reflection of the uneven development of capitalism and growth of the working class on a world scale in the latter half of the nineteenth century and the beginning of the twentieth. Membership in the Second International was limited almost entirely to European and North American workers parties.

The international workers movement paid a big overhead for this limitation. The composition of the Second International made it harder to resist the growing cancer of racism and apologies for colonialism that wracked major components of it in those years. Lenin always combated this and told the truth about it both while in the Second International and afterwards.

The Comintern recognized that the Russian Revolution had ushered in a new period in the world revolution. It came to the conclusion—following a report by Lenin at its Second Congress and some vigorous debate and discussion—that even the most economically backward countries could "go over to the Soviet system and, through certain stages of development, to communism, without having to pass through the capitalist stage." This was possible if soviet power based on mass organizations and delegated bodies of workers and peasants were established, if the working class exercised leadership in the struggle for national liberation, and if the Soviet government in Russia came to the assistance of such revolutionary regimes "with all the means at its disposal."[17]

No country in the world, the Comintern said, was doomed to inevitable and indefinite capitalist development with its attendant horrors. The victory of the Bolsheviks and its consequences had put the socialist revolution on the agenda, not just in the industrially advanced countries or a handful of the most developed colonial countries, but worldwide. It was possible to make the revolution—not guaranteed, not easy; in fact, very difficult. But it was possible. This could now be seen.

With that perspective in mind, the Comintern threw its energies into becoming a truly *world* communist organization. Proletarian Marxist parties could and must be built in *every* country.

Lenin pointed out in his opening speech to the second Comintern congress that this gathering "merits the title of a World Congress," because "we have here quite a number of representatives of the revolutionary movement in the colonial and backward countries."[18] The statutes adopted by that congress proclaimed that the Comintern "breaks once and for all with the traditions of the Second International which, in reality recognized the existence only of people with white skin." It continues, "People of white, yellow, and black skin color—the toilers of the whole earth—are fraternally united in the ranks of the Communist International."[19]

The Comintern leaders never denied the difficulties involved in this perspective of building a world party and extending the world socialist revolution. But they had confidence in the working class, which had shown what it could accomplish in October 1917. That confidence has been borne out by the subsequent sixty years of this century, as the events in Central America and the Caribbean demonstrate. The Bolshevik-led workers and peasants of Russia had opened the epoch of the world socialist revolution against imperialism—*our epoch*.

In presenting this integrated view of the world socialist revolution, the Comintern recognized and analyzed both the differences and the interrelationship between the struggle of the toilers of the colonies and oppressed nations for liberation, and that of the proletariat and its allies in the economically advanced capitalist countries.

Unless workers and their organizations in the imperialist countries gave active and unconditional support to national liberation struggles, above all those in the nations oppressed by their own governments, then revolutionary parties could not be built in those imperialist countries. The young proletariat in the oppressed nations would be hindered in coming to the fore of anti-imperialist struggles, and the world revolution could not move forward. The Bolshevik leadership of the Comintern also recognized the necessity of forging the strongest possible alliance of the new Soviet state and the oppressed nations in the struggle against imperialism.

The Comintern leaders were convinced, as Lenin explained at the Third Congress in 1921, that "the movement of the majority of the population of the globe, initially directed towards national liberation, will turn against capitalism and imperialism and will . . . play a very important revolutionary part in the coming phase of the world revolution."[20] That expectation has certainly been confirmed by the following decades of world history.

The specific characteristics of the revolution in Russia contributed to the Bolsheviks' understanding of this question and its importance. While Russia had emerged as an imperialist power at the end of the nineteenth century, the big majority of its population remained peasants. Russia remained encumbered by monarchism and holdovers from feudalism in all spheres of economic, social, and political life. This made Russia imperialism's weakest link and gave the revolution there many characteristics in common with revolutions in oppressed nations.

During the last quarter of the nineteenth century, Marx and Engels, encouraged by the outbreak of struggles by peasants and the revolutionary populist movement in Russia, foresaw the possibility that a democratic revolution against tsarist autocracy could provide a profound stimulus to revolutionary struggles by workers in western Europe. They did not even rule out that, under conditions of accompanying victories in Europe, a revolution in Russia could develop further and faster than might seem probable given the country's social, economic, and political backwardness.

Few in the international workers movement, however, had thought before 1917 that there was much chance that the first successful socialist revolution would occur in Russia. But that's what happened. And Lenin insisted that the workers movement of every country, including the most economically advanced, had a great deal to learn from the Russian experience.

"After the victory of the proletarian revolution in at least one of the advanced countries . . . Russia will soon after cease to be the model country," Lenin wrote in 1920. "At the present moment in history, however. . . the Russian model reveals to *all* countries something, and something highly significant, of their near and inevitable future."[21]

The Comintern taught us that the democratic, anti-imperialist, agrarian revolution, and the socialist revolution are combined in the oppressed nations. It charted a course toward building anti-imperialist united fronts and fighting for proletarian leadership of them. It taught us that communists, while supporting every concrete struggle against imperialism, no matter how limited or under what leadership, have to distinguish between revolutionary national movements based on the workers and peasants, and bourgeois-dominated national movements that are an obstacle to the oppressed toilers' fight for national liberation.

The Bolshevik leadership of the Communist International stressed that the working class had to build its own independent organizations and take the leadership of the national liberation struggles, not just support or applaud them. That the workers and their vanguard party had to be the most self-sacrificing in organizing the democratic, anti-imperialist battles of the oppressed peoples as a whole.

These are among the lessons that Comrade Handal said most Latin American Communist parties had so long disregarded.

The Communist International also worked hard at developing a transitional program and strategy, especially at its Third and Fourth congresses in 1921 and 1922. The majority of the leaders of the Second International, following the death of Engels in 1895, allowed a larger and larger chasm to develop between day-to-day activity around the workers' immediate and democratic demands (what they called the "minimum program") and the education and organization of the working class to make the socialist revolution and establish the dictatorship of the proletariat (the "maximum program"). The majority class-collaborationist wing of the movement limited activity to haggling for reforms within the framework of capitalism, paying verbal homage to a far-off socialist goal. Many left-wing revolutionists, in an attempt to avoid these pitfalls, ended up focusing almost exclusively on the maximum program, with little or no understanding that the struggle for immediate and democratic demands by workers, rural toilers, and oppressed nationalities is not only a powerful but also a necessary engine of revolutionary change and source of communist cadres.

The Bolsheviks in Russia, however, carried on the proletarian approach outlined in the Communist Manifesto and the political writings of Marx and Engels. In the process of preparing the Russian workers to fight for power between the February and October 1917 revolutions, Lenin and the Bolsheviks formulated a transitional program that formed a bridge between the workers' and peasants' escalating fight for immediate and democratic demands and their conquest of political power. That program and strategy enabled the proletarian vanguard to do the job.

Based on this experience, the Russian leaders of the Comintern sought to teach communists a strategy and method to avoid the minimum-maximum trap of the reformists and the self-defeating solution of the ultralefts. The Comintern revived the understanding of the need for a strategy that combines the participation and leadership by revolutionists in struggles by the workers and their allies for immediate demands and democratic rights, while advancing and explaining demands that point the way for the workers to challenge the prerogatives of the capitalists, gain greater and greater control over their own lives on the job and off, and ensure protection against exploitation and the effects of inflation and unemployment.

Most important, all this was integrated in a political perspective of advancing toward taking power, toward establishing a new government based on the workers and farmers. The toilers, led by the working class, had to overthrow the power of the property holders and establish their own government. The Comintern placed this idea at the center of its transitional strategy.

The Comintern also explained the kind of government needed by the workers to mobilize their allies and move toward the expropriation of the capitalists. It presented the fight for workers and farmers governments not simply as a popular way of expressing the socialist goal of state property and planning, but as a transitional slogan pointing toward the political instrument needed by the working class to consolidate political power; educate, organize, and mobilize the toilers; expropriate the capitalists; and begin the process of socialist construction on the basis of state property and planning. Such a government, emanating from a victorious popular revolution, opens the road to the consolidation of the dictatorship of the proletariat.

This discussion on the workers and farmers government grew out of the experiences of both successful and defeated revolutions that the generation of the Comintern had lived through—in Russia, Germany, Hungary, and elsewhere. The lessons laid out clearly there have contributed enormously to our own capacity to understand and learn from the transitional governments such as we saw in Cuba between mid-1959 and late 1960, and such as we see today in Nicaragua and Grenada. In our attempts to understand the revolutionary transformations in these countries, we have gone back time and again to the Comintern discussions.

Workers and farmers governments are characterized by a stage in the class struggle where capitalist property relations have not yet been abolished, but where the workers and farmers have conquered political power through a genuine revolution. The main task of proletarian revolutionists in such a government is to organize, mobilize, and raise the class consciousness of the working class and it allies, to lead them through the class struggle to the expropriation of the bourgeoisie and the consolidation of a workers state.

The Bolshevik leaders of the Comintern were convinced that the tempo of this transition period would be determined by the objective conditions, relationship of class forces at home and abroad, and the level of organization and preparation of the working class and its leadership.

The proletariat and poor peasants of Soviet Russia had been forced to expropriate the bourgeoisie and come into conflict with the better-off sections of the peasantry much more rapidly than originally planned. These steps were imposed on the Soviet republic in mid-1918 by major imperialist invasions and the outbreak of civil war. The proletariat of Russia paid a high price for this necessity, however. In 1921, when the bulk of the counterrevolutionary forces had been defeated, the Soviet leadership led a retreat from these earlier policies. This was the New Economic Policy (NEP). Forced requisition of grain from the peasants, necessitated by wartime demands for food for the army and urban workers, was now replaced by an established grain tax; the peasants could keep the remainder of their produce for use of their families or sale on the market. The NEP also included measures to help revive industrial production, which had been badly disrupted during the civil war. The decision was made to lease the use of certain nationalized factories, mines, forests, and oilfields to foreign capitalists and to some remaining entrepreneurs in Russia itself.

As both Lenin and Trotsky explained at the third and fourth Comintern congresses, many other revolutions would have to follow policies similar to those adopted during Russia's NEP. If they were fortunate, however, future revolutions would not be forced to do so as a retreat, as had been the case in Soviet Russia, but could do it as a less wrenching and costly transition from the outset.

Instant wholesale expropriations were not the best way for the working class to prepare itself to administer the economy all the way from the factory level to national planning. The least costly pace and priorities in each particular situation depended on leading the class struggle of the workers in the cities and the agricultural workers and poor peasants in the countryside; promoting and organizing the unions and other mass organizations, steeling the toilers against counterrevolution inside and outside the country, maintaining and expanding production to meet the needs of the people and to fund major new construction, and so on.

"We shall make as many concessions as possible within the limits, of course, of what the proletariat *can* concede and yet remain the ruling class," Lenin wrote, explaining the NEP.[22] As long as the proletariat solidly maintained its alliance with the poor peasants and layers of the middle peasantry and held on to power, great flexibility could be employed in organizing the transition from capitalism to socialism.

The Comintern didn't try to predict the particular form that a workers and farmers government would take. The key was that it would be based on an alliance of exploited classes—an alliance of the proletariat, a differentiated class, with the peasantry, a substantially more differentiated spectrum of classes.

Without that alliance, the revolution could not be successful. Lenin stressed that this was important not only for countries such as Russia, where the peasantry made up the vast majority of the population, but for industrially advanced countries as well. This was true despite big differences in the size of the working class relative to that of the peasantry, and in class relations and forms of land ownership in the countryside. The working class in every country had to develop a program and strategy to forge an alliance with potential allies among other exploited toilers, above all those on the land.

Following the severe stroke that ended Lenin's political life in March 1923 (he died at the beginning of 1924), a political struggle developed within the leadership of the Communist Party of the Soviet Union. This debate reflected, in fact, a deepening class struggle that would determine whether the course laid out by the first four Comintern congresses would be preserved and applied, or eroded and eventually reversed. The Soviet republic in these years faced tremendous obstacles—the ebb of the revolutionary upsurge in Europe, which had begun in 1920 and saw a third defeat in Germany in 1923; the imperialist blockade; the continuing toll of the civil war and imperialist invasions that had resulted in widespread poverty and the loss of thousands and thousands of the most conscious, self-sacrificing workers.

These pressures made possible the consolidation of a bureaucratic caste, petty bourgeois in character and outlook, promoting its power and relative material privileges against the interests of the Soviet working class. To do this, however, the developing bureaucracy had to come up with an ideological explanation to justify a course that was in practice negating the whole program and strategy of the Comintern, which had sought to use Soviet power to deepen the revolution and to extend it internationally.

Proletarian internationalism was slowly but surely replaced by Russian national interests at the service of the privileged caste. All this culminated in the early 1930s in the degeneration beyond hope of reform of the leadership of the Soviet Communist Party and the Comintern.

This process didn't happen all at once. Trotsky led an opposition against some major political shifts—danger signs that had begun to appear by the end of 1923. A few years later, a revolutionary situation developing in China emerged as one of the first tests of the political direction of the policy now being charted for the Comintern by Stalin and Nikolai Bukharin.

Against the perspective of the working class, in alliance with the peasant masses, playing the leading political role, which was the perspective adopted by the Comintern at its Second Congress in 1920 and reaffirmed at the subsequent two congresses, Stalin and Bukharin began in 1927 to project what they called a "bloc of four classes" to advance the Chinese revolution. As Leon Trotsky wrote some time later, "The fundamental idea of the Stalinists was to transform the Chinese bourgeoisie into a leader of the national revolution"[23]—specifically, China's leading bourgeois party, the Kuomintang, headed by Gen. Chiang Kai-shek.

To openly call for reliance on a wing of the bourgeoisie and defend that as the Comintern perspective would have been too brazen a break with its program and that of the Russian Communist Party. Instead, Stalin claimed that the Kuomintang was actually a "workers and peasants party," not a bourgeois-nationalist party. Contrary to all previous Comintern resolutions on the national and colonial question, Stalin ordered the inexperienced and young Chinese CP to give up its political and organizational independence before entering Chiang's party. The CP cadres were instructed to accept Chiang's political leadership and to agree not to differentiate themselves from, let alone criticize, the Kuomintang's bourgeois program and strategy, even though these were an obstacle to the democratic revolution against imperialist domination, landlordism, and warlordism in China.

In order not to antagonize the Kuomintang's capitalist supporters, many of whom were also big landowners, Stalin ordered the Chinese CP to renounce the organization of soviets—workers and peasants councils—in the city and countryside, to put the brakes on peasant struggles for agrarian reform, and where possible to encourage settlement by arbitration when workers came into conflict with their bosses.

In this way, not only was the proletarian party subordinated to the bourgeois misleadership of the revolution, but the worker and peasant struggles, which were key to victory, were straitjacketed. The best militants were slowly demoralized.

The bitter fruits of this class-collaborationist policy were harvested in April 1927. Under Chinese CP leadership, the workers of Shanghai had thrown off control by the reactionary feudal warlords and established their own power in that city. The Stalin leadership of the Comintern, however, ordered the CP to welcome Chiang's army into Shanghai and to disarm the Chinese workers. Frightened by the power and independence displayed by the Chinese working class in taking Shanghai, Chiang's army brutally slaughtered thousands of workers, crushed the unions, and imposed a military dictatorship defending the property and class interests of the bourgeoisie.

Having learned nothing from this disaster, Stalin then urged the CP to throw in its lot with an alleged left wing inside the bourgeois leadership of the Kuomintang, leading quickly to another lost opportunity and another massacre of workers in the city of Wuhan the following month.

Previously, in 1926, Trotsky had joined with Gregory Zinoviev, Lev Kamenev, and other Soviet Communist leaders in forming the United Opposition inside the party leadership to fight for the reversal of the current course on a variety of domestic and international questions.

The United Opposition correctly argued that far from being in continuity with Bolshevik policy, the course of Stalin and Bukharin in China was a revival of the Menshevik policy of: (1) rejecting the worker-peasant alliance and the leading role of the working class in that class alignment; and (2) placing a straitjacket on the struggles by the workers and peasants in order not to "scare off" the bourgeoisie. This had been the course urged by the Mensheviks for the Russian revolution up through 1917, and Mensheviks in exile in the mid-1920s hailed Stalin's policy as a welcome and "Marxist" turn by the Soviet government and Comintern.

In September 1927, several months after the defeats in Shanghai and Wuhan, the United Opposition presented an extensive platform to the Political Bureau of the Soviet Communist Party for consideration by the fifteenth party congress.[24] This platform included a section urging the return to a strategy for the Chinese revolution grounded in the positions of the party and the Comintern under Lenin's leadership.

As a result of the "fundamentally mistaken policy" of the Stalin leadership, the platform said, "there existed in China, in actual fact, no real Bolshevik Party" at the time of the decisive clash between revolution and counterrevolution earlier that year. The misleaders had pursued "the application of the Menshevik tactic in the bourgeois-democratic revolution" in China, insisting on the subordination of the workers and peasants to the supposedly revolutionary leadership of the bourgeoisie, that is, of its main party, Chiang Kai-shek's Kuomintang.

The real key to the Chinese revolution, the document said, consisted of two points.

First, "The Chinese peasantry, more oppressed than the Russian under tsarism, groaning under the yoke not only of their own but also of foreign oppressors, could rise, and did rise, more powerfully than the Russian peasantry in the revolution of 1905."

Second, the events of 1926–27 had confirmed the "slogan of 'soviets' proposed by Lenin for China as early as 1920." Such mass-based, delegated organizations in China, it said, "would have offered a form through which the forces of the peasantry could have been consolidated under the leadership of the proletariat. They would have been real institutions of the revolutionary-democratic dictatorship of the proletariat and the peasantry"—a formula used by the Bolsheviks during the 1905–17 period to describe the alliance of class forces necessary for a revolutionary victory over tsarism in Russia.

In contrast to the semi-Menshevik, anti-Bolshevik line pursued by Stalin and Bukharin, the United Opposition document said:

> The doctrine of Lenin, that a bourgeois-democratic revolution can be carried through only by a union of the working class and the peasants (under the leadership of the former) against the bourgeoisie, is not only applicable to China, and to similar colonial and semicolonial countries, but in fact indicates the only road to victory in those countries.

Again concretely applying Lenin's program on the colonial and national question adopted by the second Comintern congress, the United Opposition platform stated that—"in the present age of imperialist wars and proletarian revolutions and given the existence of the USSR"—a government of workers and peasants soviets in China would have had a chance of leading the toilers in a relatively rapid transition from the democratic to the socialist revolution.

Stalin's course, the document said, had thus run contrary to three pillars of early Comintern policy on the colonial revolution: (1) the possibility of emergence of peasants and workers soviets in countries such as China; (2) the need for political independence of proletarian communist parties in the fight for national liberation; and (3) the essential role of the worker-peasant alliance under proletarian leadership in struggling against both imperialism and the capitalist classes of their own countries.

That 1927 program of the opposition led by Trotsky, Zinoviev, and Kamenev stands up well against the test of history. It was a program aimed against imperialism and the bourgeois and landlord rulers. Its goal was to establish proletarian leadership of the democratic, anti-imperialist revolution; to maintain the workers' political independence from the Kuomintang; to cement an alliance with the peasantry as a whole in the struggle against landlordism and foreign domination; and to open the road as quickly as possible to the urban proletariat, in alliance with the agricultural wageworkers and poor peasants, beginning to take on the socialist tasks of the revolution.

This fundamental perspective was presented not only in United Opposition documents, but also in Trotsky's own articles throughout most of 1927. In April of that year, for example, he wrote that "the Chinese revolution is wholly capable of bringing to political power an alliance of the workers and peasants, under the leadership of the proletariat. This regime will be China's political link with the world revolution.

"In the course of the transitional period," Trotsky explained, "the Chinese revolution will have a genuinely democratic, worker-and-peasant character. In its economic life, commodity-capitalist relations will inevitably predominate. The political regime will be primarily directed to secure the masses as great a share as possible in the fruits of the development of the productive forces and, at the same time, in the political and cultural utilization of the resources of the state."

Trotsky continued: "The further development of this perspective—the possibility of the democratic revolution growing over into the socialist revolution—depends completely and exclusively on the course of the world revolution, and on the economic and political successes of the Soviet Union, as an integral part of the world revolution."

This revolutionary path, Trotsky said, "can be opened up only if the proletariat plays the leading role in the national democratic revolution," which requires "the complete independence of the Communist Party, and an open struggle waged by it . . . for the leadership of the working class and the hegemony in the revolution."[25]

By late 1927 and early 1928, however, Trotsky's views had begun to shift. He came to the conclusion that the United Opposition platform dealt with the Chinese revolution "very insufficiently, incompletely, and in part positively falsely."[26] What was the context of this evolution in Trotsky's thinking?

At the Fifteenth Congress of the Soviet Communist Party in December 1927, the Stalin- and Bukharin-led majority not only refused to acknowledge or fundamentally correct its errors on the Chinese revolution, but also expelled the United Opposition. In response, Zinoviev and Kamenev quickly capitulated, recanting their adherence to the Opposition platform.

Under these pressures, Trotsky reformulated his views on China in order to clarify more sharply his differences with Stalin and Bukharin. Trotsky accurately demonstrated the danger of the Stalin-Bukharin leadership's accelerating flight from the revolutionary course charted by the Comintern while Lenin was alive. At the same time, however, Trotsky introduced an erroneous leftist bias into the alternative course he projected for the Communist International. In doing so he echoed some of his differences with Lenin during the decade and a half leading up to the 1917 revolution. Before assessing Trotsky's new views on China in 1928, therefore, it is useful to look back at the pre-1917 debates in the Russian working-class movement.

Lessons of the Russian Revolution

What were Trotsky's pre-1917 views on strategy and class alliances in the Russian revolution? The most systematic presentation of them can be found in his 1906 work *Results and Prospects* and in several articles written by him between 1907 and 1909, collected in the book *1905*.[27] These works present Trotsky's view of what he and his political collaborator Alexander Helphand (Parvus), called the "permanent revolution" in Russia.

Trotsky viewed the Russian revolution as organically interconnected with the world revolution. The Russian revolution, he wrote, could kick off and help advance the proletarian revolution in western Europe. The only way to defend and advance a revolution in Russia was to extend it abroad. In this, Trotsky and Lenin were in fundamental agreement.

Trotsky held that the liberal bourgeoisie in Russia was incapable of leading the democratic revolution through to victory. The key class ally of the workers were the peasant masses, not the liberal capitalists. On this, too, Trotsky was in broad agreement with Lenin against the Mensheviks.

Although the young Russian working class was small relative to the overwhelming peasant majority, Trotsky held, it was nevertheless large in absolute numbers and concentrated in large factories in several major cities. The great unevenness of development in world history had posed in backward Russia the opportunity for the working class to take power for the first time and to hold it. If the democratic revolution against tsarism, landlordism, and medievalism and all its remnants were to be successful, he believed, the workers had to take power directly and

73

in their own name from the very outset.

No alliance of the workers and peasants, Trotsky said, could lead the democratic revolution to victory short of the workers themselves establishing workers' power, the dictatorship of the proletariat. "In the event of a decisive victory of the revolution," he wrote in *Results and Prospects*, "power will pass into the hands of that class which plays a leading role in the struggle— in other words, into the hands of the proletariat." The only possible outcome would be *"a revolutionary workers' government, the conquest of power by the Russian proletariat."*[28]

These views were qualitatively different from those of the Mensheviks and other class collaborationists. They reflected a revolutionary perspective.

Nonetheless, Trotsky's views differed from those of Lenin and the Bolsheviks. What were the differences? Above all they had to do with the character of the alliance that the working class needed to forge with the peasantry as a whole in Russia. What was the weight and place of that alliance in the workers' overall strategy to overthrow tsarism, landlordism, and take power? What was the relationship between this alliance and the fight by the workers for their own class demands and their course, together with the rural poor, toward the expropriation of the bourgeoisie and the beginning steps toward socialism?

Lenin insisted that, while not a slogan or demand, the formula "revolutionary dictatorship of the proletariat and peasantry" presented "a Marxist description of the class content of a victorious revolution" in Russia. This was in harmony with the Bolsheviks' proletarian program, strategy, and tactics for the Russian revolution.

"Our Party holds firmly to the view that the role of the proletariat is the *role of leader* in the bourgeois-democratic revolution," Lenin wrote in 1909, "that *joint actions* of the proletariat and the peasantry are essential to carry it through to victory; that unless *political power is won* by the revolutionary classes, victory is impossible."[29]

Ten years later he wrote:

Russia's backwardness merged in a peculiar way the proletarian revolution against the bourgeoisie with the peasant revolution against the landowners. That is what we started from in
October 1917, and we would not have achieved victory so easily then if we had not. As long ago as 1856, Marx spoke, in reference to Prussia, of the possibility of a peculiar combination of
proletarian revolution and peasant war. From the beginning of
1905 the Bolsheviks advocated the idea of a revolutionary-democratic dictatorship of the proletariat and the peasantry.[30]

It was above all around this question—the place and weight
that the Russian working class should assign to the combination of "the proletarian revolution against the bourgeoisie with
the peasant revolution against the landowners"—that Trotsky
and Lenin stood apart politically, and on which Lenin was proven
correct by the 1917 triumph and subsequent revolutionary experiences.

Trotsky, like Lenin, recognized the importance of the class
struggle in the countryside by the agricultural laborers and poor
peasants against the richer peasants, who often employed labor
and rented out land. The workers had a class interest in actively
supporting the rural poor in these struggles against exploiting
peasants. Unlike Lenin, however, Trotsky insisted that these class
divisions in the countryside precluded a strategy of alliance with
broad layers of the Russian peasantry as a whole and their parties.

The Bolsheviks insisted that the proletariat in Russia and its
vanguard party had to pursue such an alliance to bring down
tsarist autocracy and landlordism, while at the same time promoting the independent organization of the agricultural laborers and poor peasants—the most reliable allies of the working
class, and those most likely to remain at the workers' side as the
socialist course of the revolution deepened.

Trotsky had a less accurate perception than Lenin of the
radicalizing potential of peasant struggles in the democratic
revolution against tsarism and feudal holdovers in Russia. Writ-

ing in 1915, Trotsky polemicized with Lenin in the pages of the Paris newspaper *Nashe Slovo*.

> Today, based on the experience of the Russian Revolution and of the reaction, we can expect the *peasantry* to play a less independent, not to mention decisive, role in the development of revolutionary events than it did in 1905. To the extent that the peasantry has remained in the grip of "estate" and feudal slavery, it continues to suffer from economic and ideological disunity, political immaturity, and cultural backwardness and helplessness. Despite its elemental opposition to the old regime, in every movement the peasantry's social energy is always paralyzed by these weaknesses. They force it to halt where really revolutionary action begins.
>
> The economic and cultural progress made by the peasantry in this period has proceeded entirely along the line of bourgeois development, and has further developed the class contradictions within the peasantry itself. For the industrial proletariat, therefore, it is now—immeasurably more so than in 1905—a question of attracting to its side the rural proletariat and semiproletarian elements rather than the peasantry as an "estate." In these circumstances, the revolutionary movement acquires an incomparably less "national" and an incomparably greater "class" character than it had in 1905.[31]

Lenin responded to this 1915 article by Trotsky by pointing to its failure to recognize the need for the proletariat to combine an alliance with the peasant masses to make the democratic revolution with preparation to deepen the socialist course of the revolution once a victory over the tsar had been won.

Lenin agreed with Trotsky that "the differentiation of the peasantry has enhanced the class struggle within [the peasantry]; it has aroused very many hitherto politically dormant elements. It has drawn the rural proletariat closer to the urban proletariat."

At the same time, however, Lenin stressed that "the antagonism between the peasantry, on the one hand, and the [old order], on the other has become stronger and more acute. This is such an obvious truth that not *even* the thousands of phrases in scores of Trotsky's Paris articles will 'refute' it."

Trotsky counterposed the proletariat's alliance with the peasantry as a whole to an alliance with the rural poor. Lenin, on the other hand, pursued a course aimed at advancing the working class along a line of march that would enable it to lead the democratic revolution and be in the strongest possible position as that process unfolded to move forward toward the expropriation of the exploiters. Unlike Trotsky, Lenin presented a strategy for the transition from the democratic to the socialist revolution based on a concrete understanding of the shifting class alliances at each stage of this gigantic political, social, and economic transformation.

Concluding his polemic against Trotsky's article, Lenin wrote that the proletariat is

> fighting, and will fight valiantly, to win power for a republic, for the confiscation of the land, i.e., to win over the peasantry, make *full* use of their revolutionary powers, and get the *"non-*proletarian masses of the people" to take part in liberating *bourgeois* Russia from *military-feudal* "imperialism" (tsarism). The proletariat will at once utilize this ridding of bourgeois Russia of tsarism and the rule of the landowners, not to aid the rich peasants in their struggle against the rural workers, but to bring about the socialist revolution in alliance with the proletarians of Europe.[32]

This was the Bolsheviks' conception of the class forces and character of the Russian revolution, and the basis of the political course that culminated in the Bolshevik-led victory in 1917. It had been explained as early as 1905 in Lenin's pamphlet, *Two Tactics of Social Democracy in the Democratic Revolution.*[33] And, as Lenin often wrote following the October 1917 victory, it accurately described the unfolding and deepening of the class struggle in Russia once power had been conquered by the proletariat in alliance with the peasants.

In comparison to Trotsky's pre-1917 theory of permanent revolution, the Bolsheviks under Lenin's leadership had developed a much more complex and accurate understanding—both in theory and practice—of the contradictory and shifting worker-peasant alliance and the relationship between the democratic and socialist revolutions in Russia. Over some fifteen years leading up to the 1917 revolution, Trotsky's centrist views on class alliances and strategy were frequently reflected in centrist political positions. Trotsky's political course, unlike that charted by Lenin, could not have oriented the proletariat toward taking the leadership of the peasantry in the victory over tsarism and the bourgeois-landlord ruling classes in October 1917.

One of the most succinct and accurate assessments of the differences between Lenin and Trotsky in the pre-1917 period, and of their significance from the standpoint of future developments, was provided by Trotsky himself in a December 1926 speech to the Comintern Executive Committee. It is quite similar to other things Trotsky said and wrote beginning in late 1923, when a campaign against "Trotskyism" was opened by those who wanted to close minds to Trotsky's political struggle at that time against the reversal of Lenin's course by Stalin and others in the Russian CP leadership.

Referring to the pre-1917 period, Trotsky told the Comintern Executive Committee in 1926:

> The differences of that time when I was outside of the Bolshevik Party were quite weighty. They concerned, broadly, the concrete appraisal of class relations within Russian society and the perspective resulting from that with regard to the next revolution. On the other hand, these differences concerned the methods and ways of party-building and the relationship to Menshevism. On both these questions . . . by far not all of the comrades that are here were in the right as against me, but Comrade Lenin, his doctrine, and his party, were absolutely right as against me.

Later in that same 1926 speech, Trotsky said: "If 'permanent revolution,' insofar as it differed from the Leninist conception, was wrong, nevertheless, much in it was correct, and that is what made it possible for me to come to Bolshevism."[34]

Whatever the weaknesses of Trotsky's theory of permanent revolution relative to the Bolshevik program and strategy, it— unlike the program of the Mensheviks—was a view that could be held by genuine revolutionaries. It was in the same revolutionary camp as Lenin's, and as a result Trotsky was able to join and bring his closest comrades with him into the Bolshevik Party in mid-1917, become part of its leadership, and remain a Bolshevik for the rest of his life. Trotsky's conception was not so distant from the Bolshevik platform that his entire previous understanding of the class dynamics of the revolution had to be scrapped and replaced in order to be won to Bolshevism. The same cannot be said for those few individual Mensheviks who came to Lenin's party in 1917; they *did* have to make a fundamental and decisive break with their entire previous conception of the revolution, its leading class forces, and its goals.

The other side of Trotsky's 1926 statement is also true, however. His differences with Lenin's positions prior to 1917 were "quite weighty," and his theory of "'permanent revolution,' insofar as it differed from the Leninist conception, was wrong."

Moreover, these overall strategic differences were related to the conflicting positions that had developed over a decade and a half on important political questions. Let's review some of these strategic differences that were revealed during the period between the opening of the first imperialist world war in August 1914 and the opening of the Russian Revolution less than three years later, in February 1917.

When World War I broke out, Trotsky immediately condemned the social-patriotic capitulation of the majority of the leaders of the Socialist International, or Second International as it was often called, who lined up behind "their own" bourgeoisies in the war. Trotsky called for a struggle against "the chauvinist falsifiers of Marxism" and "to gather the forces of the Third International."[35] On these questions, which opened a chasm in the Second International, Trotsky was solidly in the revolutionary camp along with Lenin and the Bolsheviks and the German left led by Rosa Luxemburg and Karl Liebknecht.

But Trotsky's differences with Lenin persisted, even deepening on some substantial questions. His political stance and conduct throughout the early years of the war were an obstacle, not an aid, to the Bolsheviks' efforts to carve out a revolutionary proletarian wing in the Socialist International that would break decisively with the social patriots and form a new, revolutionary International. Trotsky did not stand firmly with Lenin either against the centrism of the Mensheviks, who pursued a conciliatory course toward the open social patriots and hoped to revive the Socialist International after peace was restored in Europe, or against the ultraleft sectarian errors of revolutionists such as Rosa Luxemburg on the national question and the agrarian question.

In 1915 the Bolsheviks, recognizing the strength of Trotsky's response to the war, proposed that he collaborate with them in producing a journal of the Russian internationalists. Despite more than a decade of sharp differences with Trotsky, Lenin was never factional, persistently and objectively trying to win him to a clear revolutionary line. Trotsky, however, rejected this offer. Instead, he devoted his time and energies to producing the Paris-based *Nashe Slovo* with a group calling themselves Menshevik Internationalists, such as Julius Martov, and a group of ultraleft former Bolsheviks, such as Anatoly Lunacharsky, whom Trotsky in 1912 had gathered into the so-called August Bloc. Despite their divergent political perspectives, these individuals now formed an alternative pole of attraction to the uncompromising internationalist current that Lenin and the Bolsheviks sought to construct.

Trotsky shed light on his decision to pursue this course in a sharply worded letter to the Bolsheviks in 1915, rejecting their proposal for collaboration and characterizing the Bolsheviks' course as factional and sectarian.[36] The intransigent line of Lenin, he wrote, was an obstacle to "truly uniting all internationalists, regardless of their faction origins or of this or that nuance in their internationalism." The Bolsheviks, he said, subordinate the "struggle against social patriotism to other considerations and aims" having to do with "factional or group ends not flowing out of the needs of the movement or the necessity to influence it in a revolutionary internationalist direction."

Opposing Lenin's unyielding political battle against the Mensheviks, Trotsky asserted that the actions of the Menshevik leaders in Russia since the outbreak of the war "undoubtedly represent steps forward toward political precision and revolutionary irreconcilability." Of course, Lenin's political evaluation of the Mensheviks' activity and trajectory, upon which Bolshevik tactics toward them were based, was confirmed following February 1917, when these same leaders conspired with the Russian capitalists to continue waging the war and pursuing the annexationist aims of the toppled tsarist regime.

Closely linked to this political error, Trotsky also rejected the position of Lenin and the Bolsheviks that "from the standpoint of the working class and of the toiling masses of all the nations of Russia, the defeat of the tsarist monarchy . . . would be the lesser evil."[37] In the July 1915 letter cited above, Trotsky argued that this revolutionary defeatist position "represents a fundamental connivance with the political methodology of social patriotism." In counterposition to the Bolshevik line, Trotsky advocated a strategy "of mobilizing the proletariat under the slogan of *struggle for peace*," and called for "neither defeat nor victory."

As a result of these differences, and his conciliationist stance toward the Mensheviks and other centrist forces, Trotsky refused to support the documents of the Bolshevik-led left wing at the September 1915 Zimmerwald conference, which was initiated by forces in the Socialist International who stood apart from the pro-war stance of the openly social-patriotic majority. The Zimmerwald Left fought for a line clearly advocating a new International and efforts by the workers of all countries to convert the imperialist war into a civil war against their capitalist rulers. Trotsky occupied a middle position at Zimmerwald between the left wing led by the Bolsheviks and the right wing led by the German centrists.[38]

In addition, during the war years Trotsky attempted to straddle the fence in the debate between Lenin, who strongly advocated support by the proletariat to the right of self-determination for oppressed nationalities, and Rosa Luxemburg (as well as other Polish revolutionists), who labeled this position an impermissible concession to outmoded and petty-bourgeois nationalist sentiments. While Trotsky in the pre-1917 period rejected Luxemburg's view and advocated support for the right to national self-determination, he substantially shared the Polish revolutionists' assessment that national liberation struggles had largely exhausted their potential as a force for revolutionary change.

Thus, Trotsky and Lenin responded in a sharply contrasting manner to the defeat of the 1916 Easter Rising in Dublin led by Irish nationalist freedom fighters against British colonial oppression.[39] The rebellion, in which the Irish fighters rejected the call to subordinate their struggle to British imperialism's war effort, was drowned in blood by the occupying army. In the aftermath, leaders of the Irish republican and socialist movements were executed.

Trotsky harshly condemned the British imperialist slaughter of "the heroic defenders of the Dublin barricades" and the denial of self-determination to Ireland. But he concluded from the crushing of the Easter Rising that "the historical basis for a national revolution has disappeared even in backward Ireland." Its failure, he said, was inevitable because of the lack of response by the Irish peasants, who "were guided merely by the blind egoism typical of farmers and their utter indifference to everything that happens beyond the bounds of their bits of land."

Lenin, to the contrary, believed that the Easter Rising put another nail in the coffin of the argument "that the vitality of small nations oppressed by imperialism has already been sapped, that they cannot play any role against imperialism, that support of their purely national aspirations will lead to nothing, etc." He saw the rebellion as one more example that

> *owing* to the crisis of imperialism, the flames of national revolt have flared up *both* in the colonies and in Europe, and that national sympathies and antipathies have manifested themselves in spite of the Draconian threats and measures of repression. . . .
>
> To imagine that social revolution is *conceivable* without revolts by small nations in the colonies and in Europe without revolutionary outbursts by a section of the petty bourgeoisie *with all its prejudices*, without a movement of the politically non-conscious proletarian and semi-proletarian masses against oppression by the landowners, the church, and the monarchy, against national oppression, etc.—to imagine all this is to *repudiate social revolution*.

Lenin continued bitingly,

> So one army lines up in one place and says, "We are for socialism," and another, somewhere else and says, "We are for imperialism," and that will be a social revolution! . . .
>
> Whoever expects a "pure" social revolution will *never* live to see it. Such a person pays lip-service to revolution without understanding what revolution is.

Lenin embraced the Easter Rising as an example of the power of revolutionary nationalist movements, an augury of the coming struggles and upsurges of oppressed peoples in the twentieth century. His assessment has been borne out many times over by the subsequent decades of national liberation struggles not only in Ireland, but in Africa, Asia, Latin America, and among the oppressed nationalities in the imperialist countries.

Finally, during the course of the war Trotsky became more, not less, convinced of the impossibility of an alliance between the Russian proletariat and broad layers of the peasantry. On this decisive question of the Russian revolution, Trotsky's differences with the Bolsheviks widened right up to the eve of the February 1917 revolution. Writing in January 1917, Trotsky recalled that in the 1905 revolution:

"The peasants arose and fought adroitly against their local slave-holders, yet they stopped in reverence before the all-Russian slave-holder. . . . The army was an obedient tool in the hands of Tsarism. It crushed the labor revolution in December, 1905." Moreover, Trotsky continued, repeating with more force his argument in *Nashe Slovo* from two years earlier, "there is less hope now for a revolutionary uprising of the peasantry as a whole than there was twelve years ago."[40]

Lenin's opposite perspective on this question, based on organizing the proletariat to take the leadership of a worker-peasant alliance to overthrow tsarism and landlordism, met the test of history as the revolution began to unfold less than a month after Trotsky had written these words.

Trotsky's work following the October 1917 revolution as a central leader of the Russian Communist Party and the Comintern superseded these earlier erroneous views, just as these experiences and lessons enriched, corrected, and superseded the earlier views of most who lived through them. The Russian leadership functioned under extremely difficult circumstances—imperialist intervention, blockade, civil war, and all their devastating results. They worked together to explain, defend, and expand the program and strategy developed by the Communist International during its first five years. In this collective work there were occasional differences—including important ones, such as over the Brest-Litovsk peace in 1918, the "trade union" debate in 1921, and so on. But there were no fundamental differentiations. The Bolshevik leaders functioned as a politically homogeneous cadre.

Following Lenin's final illness, however, as the battle opened over continuing to apply Comintern policy, those retreating from this revolutionary course threw up a smoke screen in order to divert the debate in the Soviet CP leadership onto the errors of Trotsky's political course before the revolution. Stalin, Bukharin, and their followers ripped statements about Trotsky by Lenin out of historical context and then projected what they labeled "Trotskyism" onto all those in the Bolshevik leadership who fought to maintain the program of Lenin and the Comintern.

Trotsky, as we've already seen, did not deny that he had been wrong as against the Bolsheviks on central political and strategic questions prior to 1917. Within the context of the Russian workers movement, Trotsky wrote in his 1924 article "Our Differences," he had played a centrist role. He stated:

> My "conciliationism" led me at many sharp turns in the road into hostile clashes with Bolshevism. Lenin's struggle against Menshevism was inevitably supplemented by a struggle against "conciliationism," which was often given the name "Trotskyism." . . .
>
> It would never even enter my head now, long after the fact, to dispute the correctness in principle and the colossal historical farsightedness of Lenin's critique of Russian "conciliationism," which in its essential features was akin to the international current of centrism.[41]

Trotsky was branded with "Trotskyism" to close minds to his defense of Bolshevism, and to camouflage the rise of something very real—"Stalinism," falsely parading as "Leninism."

Following the expulsion of the United Opposition at the end of 1927 and the capitulation to Stalin by Kamenev and Zinoviev, however, Trotsky began to shift the way he explained his differences with Lenin in the pre-1917 period. While he continued to acknowledge that his conciliationist stance toward the Mensheviks had been a serious political error, Trotsky began to argue that he had been correct on some important strategic questions, in particular those associated with his theory of permanent revolution. In my opinion, this change began a process of blurring the line of revolutionary continuity growing out of the Comintern program and strategy.

This shift by Trotsky developed primarily in the context of the ongoing debate within the Soviet CP leadership over perspectives for the Chinese revolution and the roots of the 1927 defeat. Stalin could not openly admit his break with Lenin's views, so both before and after the 1927 defeat he and Bukharin dressed up their semi-Menshevik views about the Kuomintang and the "bloc of four classes" in China by claiming they were simply applying Lenin's formula of the revolutionary democratic dictatorship of the proletariat and peasantry. They argued that the United Opposition, in advocating the call for the organization of soviets of workers and peasants in China, was actually making the ultraleft error of failing to recognize the democratic character of the revolution there. This, it was alleged, was evidence of the United Opposition's "Trotskyism."

The United Opposition, led by Trotsky, Zinoviev, and Kamenev, refuted this charge in the September 1927 platform cited earlier. "In mockery of Lenin's teaching," the United Opposition said, "Stalin asserted that the slogan of soviets in China would mean the demand for an immediate formation of the proletarian dictatorship. As a matter of fact Lenin, as long ago as the revolution of 1905, advanced the slogan of soviets as organs of the democratic dictatorship of the proletariat and the peasants."[42]

Prior to 1928, Trotsky, too, had rejected this charge. In May 1927, for example, Trotsky dismissed "the senseless contention . . . attributed to the Opposition that China now stands on the eve of a socialist dictatorship of the proletariat." Instead, he wrote, the Opposition held to Lenin's view that the victorious democratic revolution, "under favorable conditions, would begin to grow over into a socialist revolution."[43]

During the closing months of 1927 and early 1928, however, as Stalin pumped opportunist content into Lenin's formulas and slogans, Trotsky became more and more convinced that the application of the formula "revolutionary democratic dictatorship of the proletariat and peasantry" to the Chinese revolution could serve only as a bridge to Menshevik positions.

Trotsky's new assessment of these questions and their relationship to the errors in China was presented in his 1928 criticism of the disastrous Stalin-Bukharin course.[44] Trotsky had prepared this document for the Sixth Congress of the Comintern, while in internal exile in Soviet Central Asia under Stalin's orders. Trotsky was not only barred from attending the congress, but his criticisms were also suppressed there, although a few copies were given to members of the commission considering the draft program for the Comintern.

Trotsky did not yet insist in this document, as he would in the 1930s, on the correctness, as applied to the *Russian revolution*, of his own pre-1917 theory of permanent revolution. He wrote that "the myth of the 'permanent revolution' of 1905 [had been] placed in circulation in 1924 [by those who disagreed with him in the Soviet CP leadership] in order to sow confusion and bewilderment."

Trotsky's 1928 document, in fact, presented a description of the Bolsheviks' revolutionary democratic dictatorship formula that generally corresponded to Lenin's explanations in 1917 and afterwards. Trotsky wrote:

> Beginning with April, 1917, Lenin explained to his opponents who accused him of having adopted the position of the "permanent revolution," that the dictatorship of the proletariat and the peasantry was realized partially in the epoch of dual power [February–October 1917]. He explained later that this dictatorship met with its further extension during the first period of soviet power from November 1917 until July 1918, when the entire peasantry, together with the workers, effected the agrarian revolution while the working class did not as yet proceed with the confiscation of the mills and factories, but experimented with workers' control.

While this had been the dynamic of the revolutionary struggle in Russia, however, Trotsky was convinced that nothing comparable could be expected in China. *"There is not* and *will not be* any other 'democratic dictatorship' except the dictatorship exercised by the Kuomintang since 1925," he wrote.

As opposed to the situation in tsarist Russia, Trotsky continued,

> there is no caste of feudal landlords in China in opposition to the bourgeoisie. The most widespread, common, and hated exploiter in the village is the kulak-usurer, the agent of finance capital in the cities. The agrarian revolution is therefore just as much antibourgeois in character as it is antifeudal.
>
> In China there will be practically no such stage as the first stage of our October revolution, in which the kulak [rich peasant] marched with the middle and poor peasant, frequently at their head, against the landlord. . . . If in our country the poor peasant committees appeared on the scene only during the second stage of the October revolution, in the middle of 1918, in · China, on the contrary, they will, in one form or another, appear on the scene as soon as the agrarian movement revives. The drive on the rich peasant will be the first and not the second step of the Chinese October.

Here, as he had done before 1917 in relation to Russia, Trotsky recognized one crucial side of the class struggle in China—that of the struggle of the rural poor against the rich peasants. But he did so to the exclusion of seeing the need for the proletariat to forge an alliance with the broadest possible layers of the peasantry to carry through the democratic revolution and open the road to the socialist revolution. In explaining the disastrous consequences of Stalin's opportunist course and fighting to reverse it, Trotsky telescoped the stages of the revolution in China.

One of the central contentions of his 1928 document was that the Chinese revolution, "despite the great backwardness of China, or more correctly, because of this great backwardness compared with Russia, will not have a 'democratic' period, not even such a six-month period as the October revolution had (November 1917 to July 1918); but it will be compelled from the very outset to effect the most decisive shakeup and abolition of bourgeois property in city and village."

The actual course of events in China shows how erroneous Trotsky's idea was that the abolition of bourgeois property in city and countryside in China would immediately be possible upon the workers and poor peasants taking power. Following the victory of the Chinese Revolution in 1949, as we know, there *was* a period comparable to that between November 1917 and July 1918 in Russia. In fact, this period extended much longer in China than in Soviet Russia, which was forced by the civil war and imperialist intervention to foreshorten the transition.

The Chinese workers and peasants, both before and after the 1949 victory over Chiang Kai-shek, have paid a heavy price for the Maoist misleadership of their struggles. Even had a proletarian Marxist leadership stood at the head of the Chinese workers and peasants, however, a period of transition would have been necessary to prepare the workers and poor peasants to expropriate the exploiters and begin organizing production on an entirely new basis. As we've seen in subsequent revolutions, this is not an instant process.

In combating Stalin's rightist errors, Trotsky in 1928 injected leftist errors. While not directly challenging the Bolsheviks' pre-1917 strategy as applied to Russia, Trotsky in fact revived his own pre-1917 position, rejecting an alliance with the peasantry as a whole in the democratic revolution. He now applied this to China, and, by implication, to other countries in the colonial world. Trotsky's 1928 document had no concept of a transitional regime and period, based on this worker-peasant alliance. It advanced no strategy that would enable the Chinese workers to gain experience and lead their most consistent allies, the agricultural wageworkers and poor peasants, in the expropriation of the exploiters and the establishment of new relations of production based on state property and planning.

In sharp contrast to his rejection of any transitional period or regime in the 1928 document, Trotsky had written in 1922 that a government "similar to ours in Russia when we created a workers and peasants government together with the Left Socialist-Revolutionaries . . . would constitute a transition to the proletarian dictatorship, the full and completed one."[45]

Trotsky in 1928 was retreating from views that he and Lenin had held in common since the opening years of the Russian Revolution, not only on the relationship of the democratic and socialist revolutions in the colonial countries, but on another related question of revolutionary strategy. At the fourth Comintern congress in 1922, Lenin and Trotsky had explained that a New Economic Policy—a period of mixed economy of a certain kind—will be the *norm* following a revolutionary victory of workers allied with rebelling peasants.

Only "the implacable demands of the Civil War," Trotsky said at this congress, obliged the Soviet republic "to expropriate the bourgeoisie at one blow, to destroy the bourgeois economic apparatus and to replace the latter hastily by the apparatus of War Communism."[46] The workers and peasants paid a heavy price for this, as both Lenin and Trotsky explained.

Yet by 1928, Trotsky had come not only to expect, but to advocate, such a hasty transition "at one blow" for the revolution in China—a country even more heavily burdened by precapitalist social relations than was Russia under the tsar.

Trotsky had also explained in 1922, referring to the discussion on the workers and peasants government slogan at the fourth Comintern congress, that the "great value of this slogan for us" is that it is "a *stage* toward the dictatorship of the proletariat."[47]

It is to Trotsky's 1928 critique of Stalin's anti-Marxist course with its leftist weaknesses, that the international movement of which we in the Socialist Workers Party are part traces its birth as an organized international political current. That document, not the platform of the earlier United Opposition, is what James P. Cannon and Maurice Spector got hold of while attending the sixth Comintern congress in 1928, and around which the initial cadres of our movement in North America and internationally were subsequently gathered and educated.

The political heart of that document is something we still base ourselves on and learn from each time we study it—a powerful defense of the proletarian internationalist outlook of Marx, Engels, and Lenin against Stalin's course toward abandoning it and replacing it with a narrow Russian nationalist outlook reflecting the interests of the crystallizing privileged bureaucracy.

Cuban Communist Party leader Fidel Castro, in reporting on the party's founding program at its First Congress in 1975, said, "The starting point of Cuba's foreign policy . . . is the subordination of Cuban positions to the internationalist needs of the struggle for socialism and for the national liberation of the peoples."[48] That was the position that Trotsky in 1928 was fighting to revive as the starting point for the Soviet Communist Party, and for the Communist International.

Trotsky's 1928 document correctly rejected Stalin's course toward subordinating the Chinese proletariat and peasantry to the misleadership of the bourgeois Kuomintang—a policy that had led to crushing defeats the previous year.

The document, however, also contained leftist errors, as we've seen. Our movement has been educated on those parts of the document, as well. Most of these weaknesses were later corrected by Trotsky in practice. But neither Trotsky while he was alive nor—to my knowledge—anyone in the leadership of our movement has ever taken issue with those sections before. We have never pointed to them as contrary to our overall course, which they are. They are contrary to our programmatic continuity with Lenin, and contrary to the lessons from actual revolutions, led by proletarian revolutionists, since World War II.

The problem this poses for us, for communists in the 1980s, is not simply that we've stumbled across some historical or theoretical inconsistency. The problem is that the actual course of the revolutionary class struggle has convinced us that we must fully reconquer the program and strategy of the early Comintern, which incorporated and built on Lenin's course carried out by the Bolsheviks culminating in the October 1917 victory.

We can't do that, however, unless we disentangle this central core of our political continuity from the leftist bias brought in by the erroneous side of Trotsky's pre-1917 views, including those revived by Trotsky in the 1928 document. We have to explain truthfully, frankly, without self-serving apologies, and to the end, where Trotsky fits into the revolutionary continuity we trace through Marx, Engels, Lenin, the Bolshevik Party, and the first four congresses of the Communist International.

Our answer, in my opinion, has to be that Trotsky's place in our revolutionary programmatic continuity begins in mid-1917 when he became part of the Bolshevik leadership that organized the October 1917 revolution. Before that, of course, Trotsky was already a revolutionary who had played an important and courageous role in the 1905 revolution and other battles of the Russian workers movement. In that broader sense, he is part of our revolutionary continuity, as are Rosa Luxemburg and many other revolutionary fighters and leaders.

But we are talking about something more specific—our programmatic continuity. From that standpoint, Trotsky's place begins when he becomes a Bolshevik. That is where our Trotsky begins.

An irreplaceable programmatic heritage

The Bolshevik Party's Central Committee was the result of a successful fusion of forces into that party in the months preceding October 1917. Working together with Lenin and under his leadership, Trotsky helped develop many of the strategic and programmatic guidelines of the Comintern, the Soviet Communist Party, and the Soviet state. Lenin's success in drawing Trotsky into the Bolshevik Party leadership was an important accomplishment. It not only benefited the revolution, but—as it turned out—it brought into the central Soviet leadership the one member who after 1928 was able to continue the battle for over a decade to maintain the Bolshevik course.

In 1933, following Hitler's devastating seizure of power in Germany and the default of the Comintern in face of this disaster, it became clear that reform of the Stalinist-led Communist International was no longer possible. A new International was necessary. Trotsky was insistent, however, that there was no parallel necessity to lay a new theoretical foundation, to develop a new program and strategy.

Trotsky's writings throughout the 1930s on the colonial revolution, the Black struggle, the battle against fascism in Germany and Spain, how the workers movement can develop a transitional program and strategy, the proletarianization of the communist movement—all these were aspects of his struggle to defend and maintain the political ground conquered by the Comintern during its first five years. Of course, maintaining those conquests meant attempting to implement and enrich them in the light of new experiences in the class struggle.

A glimpse into Trotsky's approach to the Comintern legacy during this period is provided by an incident described in a book written several years ago by Jean Van Heijenoort, one of Trotsky's secretaries from 1932 to 1939.[49] Van Heijenoort recalls that when Trotsky came to the conclusion in his own mind about the necessity for a new International, one of the first things he did was to ask Van Heijenoort and another secretary—Pierre Frank, who unlike Van Heijenoort remains a revolutionary in the Fourth International today—to pull together all the theses and resolutions adopted by the first four Comintern congresses. He was determined to put those forward as the foundations of the program of the new International.

Here is what Trotsky himself had to say about this question in August 1933, the month the formal decision was adopted to chart a course toward a new International:

> The first four congresses of the Communist International left us an invaluable programmatic heritage: the character of the modern epoch as an epoch of imperialism, that is, of capitalist decline; the nature of modern reformism and the methods of struggle with it; the relation between democracy and proletarian dictatorship; the role of the party in the proletarian revolution; the relation between the proletariat and the petty bourgeoisie, especially the peasantry (the agrarian question); the problem of nationalities and the liberation struggle of colonial peoples; work in the trade unions; the policy of the united front; the relation to parliamentarism, etc.—all these questions have been subjected by the first four congresses to a principled analysis that has remained unsurpassed until now.

Trotsky continued:

> One of the first, most urgent tasks of those organizations that have inscribed on their banners the regeneration of the revolutionary movement consists in separating out the principled decisions of the first four congresses, in bringing them

in order and in subjecting them to a serious discussion in the light of the future tasks of the proletariat.[50]

Around this time, in December 1933, the leadership of the International Left Opposition in Europe, where Trotsky was living in exile, sent a letter to the Communist League of America, one of the predecessors of the SWP, asking that we consider publishing the material from the first four Comintern congresses. The CLA's national committee voted to undertake the project and to ask Trotsky to write an introduction to it. The project, however, was never carried out.

The new International did not have a new name. It was simply called the Fourth International, the world party of socialist revolution. Its goal was to contribute to the process of building a mass world party, a revolutionary proletarian International such as the Comintern had set out to construct.

Its founding document, which has become known as the Transitional Program, was drafted by Trotsky. It explained that since 1917 there have been three sectors of the world revolution—not just the imperialist countries and the oppressed colonial and semicolonial world, but also a workers state.

In 1938 there was only one workers state, the Soviet Union. The revolution that had given birth to that state had degenerated. A bureaucratic caste had usurped political power from the working class, and this privileged layer had to be replaced by the workers through a political revolution. But the Fourth International unconditionally defended that workers state—that gigantic conquest of the world proletariat—against imperialism and capitalist restoration. A resolution of its May 1940 emergency conference declared:

> The class conscious worker knows that a successful struggle for complete emancipation is unthinkable without the defense of conquests already gained, however modest. All the more obligatory therefore is the defense of so colossal a conquest as planned economy against the restoration of capitalist relations.

Those who cannot defend old positions will never conquer new ones.[51]

Trotsky saw that the three sectors of the world revolution, while each has important strategic problems of its own, are parts of a single complex and contradictory process of class struggle against the imperialist ruling classes and their international system of exploitation and oppression. While the program and strategy for each sector differ according to the property and class relations that prevail in them, the revolutionary proletariat in all three sectors is united around the common overriding goal of overthrowing world imperialism.

Trotsky's last political battle, before his death in 1940 at the hands of Stalin's assassins, was against those in the Fourth International who—demoralized by the approaching world war, disoriented by Stalin's crimes, and resisting a turn toward the industrial working class—were buckling to imperialist pressure and middle-class radical opinion by abandoning defense of the Soviet workers state. Trotsky insisted that these people, whom he correctly described as the "petty-bourgeois opposition," had given up the perspective of an integrated, worldwide struggle against imperialism. They had lost sight of the fact that the struggle against the Stalinist bureaucracy in the USSR, while a component of the world anticapitalist struggle, was at the same time subordinate to defense of the workers' conquests against imperialism. As Trotsky wrote in late 1939:

> We must formulate our slogans in such a way that the work-
> ers see clearly just what we are defending in the USSR (state
> property and planned economy), and against whom we are con-
> ducting a ruthless struggle (the parasitic bureaucracy and its
> Comintern). We must not lose sight for a single moment of the
> fact that the question of overthrowing the Soviet bureaucracy
> is for us subordinate to the question of preserving state prop-
> erty in the means of production in the USSR; that the question
> of preserving state property in the means of production in the

USSR is subordinate for us to the question of the world proletarian revolution.[52]

Following the path blazed by the Communist International, Trotsky was also firmly committed to building a truly *world* revolutionary movement. A 1940 resolution of the Fourth International explained that, together with the struggle of the working class in the imperialist countries, the struggle for national liberation "represents one of the two great progressive forces in modern society."[53]

"We can and we must find a way to the consciousness of the Negro workers, the Chinese workers, the Indian workers, and all the oppressed in the human ocean of the colored races," Trotsky wrote, "to whom belongs the decisive word in the development of mankind."[54]

"The movement of the colored races against their imperialist oppressors is one of the most important and powerful movements against the existing order," Trotsky emphasized on the ninetieth anniversary of the Communist Manifesto, "and therefore calls for the complete, unconditional, and unlimited support on the part of the proletariat of the white race. The credit for developing revolutionary strategy for oppressed nationalities belongs primarily to Lenin."[55]

Trotsky also carried on the Comintern's work of educating revolutionists in the United States about the centrality of the struggle for Black self-determination and of the vanguard role of Black workers in the class struggle. Transcripts of his discussions on this question with leaders of our movement in the 1930s are collected in the book *Leon Trotsky on Black Nationalism and Self-Determination.*[56]

It was during one of those discussions that Trotsky made clear, in very vivid language, the intransigent spirit in which a revolutionized mass labor movement would approach racism and racist violence in this country. For every lynching, Trotsky said, ten or twenty lynchers should be lynched.

Trotsky also waged a political battle within the Fourth International during the last years of his life to proletarianize its various national parties, to convince them to turn their entire leadership and membership toward the industrial working class. "Trotsky's perpetual grievance against the Trotskyite groups was their poor social composition," his former secretary Van Heijenoort recalls, "too many intellectuals, too few workers."[57]

It was absolutely essential to alter this social composition, Trotsky insisted, both to take advantage of opportunities created by the workers' radicalization under the hammerblows of the international capitalist crisis in the 1930s, and to withstand the intense pressures bearing down on the workers and their allies as a result of the approaching imperialist world war.

The weight of petty-bourgeois elements in the Fourth International, Trotsky believed, was responsible for the development of the current that rejected defense of the Soviet Union.

In party building, as in other things, Trotsky based himself on the lessons he learned from Lenin, fighting for parties proletarian in composition and leadership that are part of a mass communist International. That was Trotsky's goal.

The conditions under which our movement fought for this goal got tougher and tougher, as our class sustained mighty blows in the 1930s—fascist victories in Germany and Spain, the tightening grip of the Stalinists and Social Democrats on the mass workers' organizations. These defeats, which culminated in World War II, took a tremendous toll on the international labor movement.

Throughout the 1930s our movement had responded to any sign of proletarian resistance in the traditional workers' organizations, seeking to link up with forces moving toward communism. By the end of the decade some important gains had been made and some centrist obstacles gotten out of the way. But no currents with a mass following had broken in a revolutionary direction. Under a death sentence from Stalin during the last years of his life, Trotsky wrote in the founding program of the new International that outside of our own small cadres, "there does not exist a single revolutionary current on this planet really meriting the name."[58] That was the fact in 1938.

But Trotsky never lost confidence in the working class. His confidence was rooted in his materialist outlook, his Marxist understanding of the world, confirmed in his own experience by the October Revolution in Russia. The big majority of the proletarian cadres of the International Left Opposition stood firm on this revolutionary perspective, as well. The same cannot be said about all of those in and around the Trotskyist movement in those years, however.

Take Jean Van Heijenoort, for example, whose book, *With Trotsky in Exile,* I cited earlier. In 1948 he turned his back on Marxism and the communist movement. At the end of the book, Van Heijenoort explains his political evolution after he left Trotsky's staff in 1939:

> For seven years following Trotsky's death I remained active in the Trotskyite movement. By 1948 the Marxist-Leninist ideas about the role of the proletariat and its political capacity seemed more and more to me to disagree with reality. This was also the time when the full extent of Stalin's universe of concentration camps became known, at least to those who did not wish to close their eyes or stop their ears. Under the impact of this revelation, I began to reexamine the past, and I came to ask myself whether the Bolsheviks, by establishing an irreversible police rule and obliterating all public opinion, had not prepared the soil on which the huge and poisonous mushroom of Stalinism had grown. . . . Bolshevik ideology was, for me, in ruins.[59]

Van Heijenoort was certainly in ruins, politically. Bolshevik ideology is another question.

What is so revealing about this passage are the two things that Van Heijenoort remembers as the cause of his break with Marxism.

First, he could not maintain a commitment to defend the Soviet Union as a conquest of the workers of the world, regardless of the depth of the problems of bureaucratic misrule. Instead, he became convinced that the October Revolution, Bolshevism, and Lenin were themselves the source of the problem.

Second, Van Heijenoort said he had given the working class exactly 100 years to produce socialism. That was enough. By 1948, he was convinced that the workers could not and would not accomplish anything in history.

Van Heijenoort, and others like him, thus turned their backs on the two most important conquests from Comintern experience, from the Bolshevik Party, and from Lenin—if you have to single out two—that Trotsky fought to develop and instill in the young workers being won to the Fourth International.

This, then, is *our* Trotsky—the continuator and enricher of the revolutionary continuity of communism. Trotsky, from mid-1917 on a leader of the Soviet Communist Party, part of the Russian leadership of the Communist International, one of the central leaders of the Soviet state, commander of the Red Army.

And Trotsky, together with other Russian Communist leaders in the 1920s, was part of the fight to reverse the retreat from the revolutionary course charted while Lenin was still alive. Trotsky, alone in the 1930s among the Bolsheviks who had led the Communist International during its first five years, continued the fight to defend and extend the world socialist revolution and build proletarian communist parties as part of a world movement.

While Trotsky fought to continue the program and strategy of Lenin and the Comintern during his final exile the last twelve years of his life, he simultaneously came to insist on the erroneous character of Lenin's formula of the revolutionary democratic dictatorship of the proletariat and the peasantry in the pre-1917 period in Russia, and on the correctness of his own alternative to it during those years.

In important articles such as "Three Conceptions of the Russian Revolution,"[60] written during the final year of his life, as well as in many other writings throughout the 1930s, Trotsky argued that the events of 1917 had shown in practice that the real continuity of the program and strategy of the Russian Communist Party and the Comintern went back to the theory of permanent revolution he had argued for in the years before the revolution. In the context of world developments in the 1930s, Trotsky believed, Lenin's formula was so open to misinterpretation that it facilitated the influence of Stalinist class-collaborationism in the ranks of the world Communist movement.

Trotsky did acknowledge during his final exile that some of his own writings in the pre-1917 period had also contained characterizations of the class dynamics of the Russian Revolution that were shown to be wrong by actual events in 1917–18. He stressed that these were the result of polemical excess inevitable in any political debate, however, not fundamental weaknesses of his theory of permanent revolution.

For example, in Trotsky's 1929 work entitled "The Permanent Revolution," he wrote, "Articles can be found in which I expressed doubts about the future revolutionary role of the peasantry *as a whole, as an estate,* and in connection with this refused to designate, especially during the imperialist war, the future Russian revolution as 'national,' for I felt this designation to be ambiguous." Two such articles by Trotsky, from 1915 and January 1917, have been cited earlier.

Acknowledging the error of these statements, Trotsky continued that "it must not be forgotten here that the historical processes that interest us, including the processes in the peasantry, are far more obvious now that they have been accomplished than they were in those days when they were only developing."[61]

That understanding of the weight and role of the peasantry in the Russian Revolution, however, had been at the very center of Bolshevik strategy. And it was the decisive question on which Lenin's views were correct as against Trotsky's theory of permanent revolution, laying the basis for the political course around which the Bolshevik Party was built.

This acknowledgment by Trotsky of his error on this question is important. It shows the lasting impact of lessons he had learned about the worker-peasant alliance from his experience after 1917 under Lenin's guidance as a leader of the Russian Revolution, Soviet state, and Communist International.

Nonetheless, Trotsky's post-1927 return to his view that he had been correct against the Bolsheviks on some of the important strategic questions in the pre-1917 period is not just a historical question. It has not been without negative political results in the Fourth International, and for that reason especially merits serious discussion by us today. How did Trotsky explain these early differences with Lenin?

In his 1938 article, "Revolution and War in China,"[62] Trotsky put it this way: "The weak point of Lenin's conception was the internally contradictory idea of the 'bourgeois-democratic dictatorship of the proletariat and peasantry.' A political bloc of two classes whose interests only partially coincide excludes a dictatorship."

Trotsky viewed this algebraic character of Lenin's formula to be its weak point. That was its strength, however. Lenin was completely aware of the social contradictions bound up in the revolutionary process he sought to capture in his formula. He was completely aware that the proletariat and peasantry were classes "whose interests only partially coincide." The key to proletarian strategy in Russia was to forge a worker-peasant alliance around those interests that *did* coincide—that is, around the fight to bring down absolutism and landlordism—and to establish a dictatorship based on that alliance to carry out those democratic tasks while opening the door to the socialist revolution. The Bolshevik formula was exactly the kind of algebraic approach needed to orient the proletariat in practice, in action, toward leading an alliance of exploited classes through the transition from a victorious democratic revolution to the establishment and consolidation of a workers state.

Trotsky continued: "Lenin himself emphasized the fundamental limitation of the 'dictatorship of the proletariat and peasantry' when he openly called it *bourgeois*." (I should point out here that although Trotsky repeatedly refers to the "bourgeois democratic dictatorship" in this article, Lenin referred to the "revolutionary democratic dictatorship," or sometimes just the "democratic dictatorship." The difference is not unimportant.)

Continuing with Trotsky's point: "By this [Lenin] meant to say that for the sake of maintaining the alliance with the peasantry the proletariat would, in the coming revolution, have to forego the direct posing of socialist tasks."

But this was not Lenin's position. The question was not one of the proletariat foregoing socialist tasks in order to maintain an alliance with the peasantry. It was how to successfully carry through with those tasks. The question was how the proletariat could weld a fighting alliance with the peasantry *in order to* overthrow tsarism and landlordism and use the resulting governmental power to carry out the democratic revolution, while at the same time beginning to grapple with the socialist tasks, important elements of which would be posed from the outset. The tempo of the transition as a whole would be determined concretely by the relationship of class forces at home and abroad, the level of organization and consciousness of the workers and poor peasants, and the material conditions in the country.

Trotsky goes on: "Lenin, influenced by historical experience, had acknowledged [this formula] to be without value."

"In other words," Trotsky said, "the Comintern picked up a formula discarded by Lenin only in order to open the road to the politics" of Menshevism.

These statements by Trotsky about Lenin's post-1917 views are, I believe, factually incorrect. I don't doubt that Trotsky had come to believe them to be true. Much of Trotsky's library and files, which he used to verify facts, fell victim to Stalinist thefts and to other losses, as he was hounded from country to country by bourgeois governments and the Moscow bureaucracy during his final exile. He was often dependent on archive materials and translations provided by John G. Wright, a leader of our movement here in the United States.

Whatever the source of the error, however, Trotsky was wrong in asserting that Lenin had "discarded" the formula of the revolutionary democratic dictatorship of the proletariat and peasantry or "acknowledged it to be without value." I have heard of no one who has pointed to such statements anywhere in Lenin's published works.

Lenin did say in April 1917 that advocating the revolutionary democratic dictatorship no longer corresponded to the tasks of the day in Russia. It had already been partially realized in the formation of the soviets, Lenin said, and the task now was to concentrate on fighting for the soviets to take power, instead of ceding it to the bourgeoisie, as the class-collaborationist misleaders were doing. By taking power, the toilers would have the necessary instrument they needed to accelerate carrying out the tasks of the revolutionary democratic dictatorship.

But the basic approach to the class alliance that *could* establish a revolutionary government was never rejected or repudiated by Lenin. To the contrary, he insisted time and again from 1917 on that it was this strategy and the political course flowing from it that made possible the victory of the October Revolution.

In fact, throughout most of 1927, Trotsky himself used Lenin's formula in his own writings on the Chinese revolution. He correctly pointed to it as the Marxist alternative to the line Stalin and Bukharin were then carrying out as the course that corresponded to the needs of the Chinese workers and peasants. Lenin's formula was also used in the platform of the United Opposition. This would not have been so if either Trotsky or others in the Soviet Communist Party leadership during these years believed that Lenin had come to the conclusion a decade earlier that the formula was without value and had been discarded, even in regard to Russia.

Far from having given up the Bolsheviks' pre-1917 strategy, the continuity of this conception was embodied in the 1919 program of the Russian Communist Party and in the program of the Comintern. As pointed out previously, Lenin had referred to the revolutionary democratic dictatorship as a "Marxist description of the class content of a victorious revolution." Since the Russian Revolution had given a specific organizational form to that class alliance—the soviets of workers' and peasants' and soldiers' deputies—he incorporated *this* perspective into the speeches and resolutions he wrote for the Comintern on the revolution in the colonial world, not his pre-1917 formula. This was not because it had been proven wrong and "too algebraic," but because it had been realized in the course of a revolution, and the "algebra" could therefore be given greater concreteness. The concept of soviets—mass, delegated bodies of the toilers—had set an example around the world for revolutionary-minded workers and peasants.

The workers and farmers government

The Comintern at its Fourth Congress in 1922 adopted the transitional slogan of the workers, or workers and peasants, government for use by communists in every country to help us emulate what the revolutionary toilers of Russia had done in establishing Soviet power. It is this perspective that we have found so useful in helping us understand the socialist revolutions since World War II. On the basis of those experiences, we have been able to give greater concreteness to this slogan and have placed it at the center of our program and strategy today for both the imperialist and oppressed countries.[63]

This slogan is more useful for us today than the Bolsheviks' pre-1917 formula, since it is based on decades of historical experience and lessons since Lenin's day with victorious, and with defeated, revolutions. At the same time, we have found that our understanding of the workers and farmers government slogan, along with our ability to apply it in the class struggle, has been greatly enriched by our intensive study over the past two years of Lenin's writings from the pre-1917 period. Our use of the workers and farmers government slogan today is rooted just as much in the lessons from the Bolshevik program and strategy explained by Lenin as it is in the later Comintern discussions, which were themselves based on that same programmatic continuity.

From the late 1920s through the early 1930s, Trotsky had rejected use of the workers and farmers government slogan by communists. This was during a period in which Stalin was twisting the content of this slogan along the same class-collaborationist lines that he was using to put opportunist content into

Lenin's formula of the revolutionary democratic dictatorship of the proletariat and peasantry. The content that Stalin sought to give both slogans was subordination to bourgeois parties and governments, instead of organizing the workers to lead the toilers in the revolutionary fight toward seizing governmental power from the exploiters.

Trotsky reversed this position on the workers and farmers government slogan in the mid-1930s. In the Transitional Program drafted by him for the founding conference of the Fourth International he advocated its use.[64] In that 1938 document in fact, Trotsky shed some light on the evolution of his view of this slogan and of its connection with the formula of the revolutionary democratic dictatorship of the proletariat and peasantry. He wrote:

> When the Comintern [under Stalin] tried to revive the formula buried by history, the "democratic dictatorship of the proletariat and peasantry," it gave to the formula of the "workers and peasants government" a completely different, purely "democratic," i.e., bourgeois content, *counterposing* it to the dictatorship of the proletariat.
>
> The Bolshevik-Leninists resolutely rejected the slogan of the "workers and peasants government" in the bourgeois-democratic version. They affirmed then and affirm now that when the party of the proletariat refuses to step beyond bourgeois-democratic limits, its alliance with the peasantry is simply turned into a support for capital, as was the case with the Mensheviks and Socialist Revolutionaries in 1917, with the Chinese Communist Party in 1925–27, and as is now the case with the People's Front in Spain, France, and other countries.

Trotsky continued:

> The slogan "workers and peasants government" is thus acceptable to us only in the sense that it had in 1917 with the Bolsheviks, i.e., as an antibourgeois and anticapitalist slogan, but

in no case in that "democratic" sense which the [Stalinists] later gave it, transforming it from a bridge to socialist revolution into the chief barrier upon its path.

Having outlined the way communists use the slogan "for a workers and farmers government," Trotsky then turned to another question—one that had been discussed at the fourth Comintern congress, and that has become particularly important in light of developments since World War II.

"Is the creation of such a government by the traditional workers' organizations possible?" Trotsky asked.

> Past experience shows, as has already been stated, that this is, to say the least, highly improbable. However, one cannot categorically deny in advance the theoretical possibility that, under the influence of completely exceptional circumstances (war, defeat, financial crash, mass revolutionary pressure, etc.), the petty-bourgeois parties, including the Stalinists, may go further than they themselves wish along the road to a break with the bourgeoisie. In any case, one thing is not to be doubted: even if this highly improbable variant somewhere, at some time, becomes a reality and the workers and farmers government in the above-mentioned sense is established in fact, it would represent merely a short episode on the road to the actual dictatorship of the proletariat.

Thus, Trotsky not only affirmed the value of the slogan as a key part of the transitional program of a revolutionary proletarian party, but also reiterated the possibility that such a transitional government could come about. He reached these conclusions despite the continuing misuse of the term by the Stalinists.

Trotsky, however, didn't live to see the revolutions that followed World War II or the appearance of workers and farmers governments under whatever leadership. He didn't have the opportunity to incorporate these class-struggle experiences into his understanding of workers and farmers governments, as we in the Socialist Workers Party have.

Trotsky's emphasis in the Transitional Program was on the improbability of such a government. But history has now taught us to view it as "the first form of government that can be expected to appear as the result of a successful anticapitalist revolution."[65] That's how Joseph Hansen put it in 1977—summarizing lessons from postwar revolutions in Cuba, Algeria, China, and Yugoslavia. And Joe wasn't restricting this generalization to semicolonial or economically backward countries.

The view presented by Trotsky in 1938 is not the one we hold today. Ours builds on the insights of the Transitional Program, but goes further based on the concrete ways the world revolution has unfolded over the past forty-five years. We advocate workers and farmers governments. We have seen examples of how such governments can advance the mobilization and organization of the workers and their allies to carry out the expropriation of the capitalists and the establishment of new workers states.

Trotsky incorporated his views on the formula of the revolutionary democratic dictatorship of the proletariat and peasantry in the resolution he drafted for the 1933 conference of the International Left Opposition, a forerunner of the Fourth International. That document outlined eleven principles of a revolutionary International, the sixth of which was as follows:

> Rejection of the formula of the *"democratic dictatorship of the proletariat and peasantry"* as a separate regime distinguished from the *dictatorship of the proletariat,* which wins the support of the peasant and the oppressed masses in general; rejection of the anti-Marxist theory of the peaceful "growing-over" of the democratic dictatorship into the socialist one.[66]

The two sides of this brief paragraph deserve closer examination.

One side is Trotsky's defense of the position—at the center

of our communist continuity from Marx, Engels, and Lenin—
that the workers must lead their allies in a *revolution* to take
power from the old ruling classes and to establish a new state
power, a revolutionary dictatorship.

It is important to note Trotsky's use of the phrase "as a separate regime distinguished from" to describe what must be rejected in the Stalinists' use of the revolutionary democratic dictatorship slogan in relation to the dictatorship of the proletariat.
This was how Stalin and his supporters did use Lenin's formula,
not to describe a revolutionary transition, as Lenin had used it.
Not as a *bridge* to the dictatorship of the proletariat, but as "a
separate regime distinguished from it" and thus an obstacle to
its achievement.

The conception—and line of action—imposed on the communist movement in Stalin's time, in fact, was the one Salvadoran leader Schafik Jorge Handal explained in his article and
rejected, one that is a barrier to the workers wresting power from
the capitalists. A line that, as Handal puts it, attempts to sever
"the essential and indissoluble connection" between the struggle
for democratic and socialist tasks, that denies they are "facets
of one revolution and not two revolutions." A line that tells the
proletariat "that the democratic revolution is not necessarily to
be organized and promoted principally by us, but that we could
limit ourselves to supporting" bourgeois and petty-bourgeois
forces that would play the leading role.

These are precisely the Stalinist negations of Marxism that
Trotsky sought to combat in the 1933 document. Trotsky was
also arguing against what Handal describes as "the idea of a
peaceful road to revolution"—a road that does not involve the
revolutionary struggle for power by the working class at the
head of its exploited allies.

This is Trotsky's fundamental point, as he explained in other
articles written around the same time. His central concern was
with the conquest of power, with the need for a revolutionary
class dictatorship, which Stalin had jettisoned.

One such article, from 1931, also makes clear that by this time

Trotsky no longer held the ultraleft view he had incorporated into his critique of the Comintern's draft program in 1928 that a victorious revolutionary government in China or other colonial countries "will be compelled from the outset to effect the most decisive shakeup and abolition of bourgeois property in city and village." He wrote in that 1931 article:[67]

> The fact is that the dictatorship of the proletariat does not at all coincide mechanically with the inception of the socialist revolution. The seizure of power by the working class occurs in definite national surroundings, in a definite period, for the solution of definite tasks.
>
> In backward nations, such *immediate* tasks have a democratic character: the national liberation from imperialist subjugation and the agrarian revolution, as in China; the agrarian revolution and the liberation of the oppressed nationalities, as in Russia. . . .
>
> Lenin even said that the proletariat in Russia came to power in October 1917 primarily as an *agent of the bourgeois-democratic revolution*. The victorious proletariat began with the solution of the democratic tasks, and only gradually, by the logic of its rule, did it take up the socialist tasks; it took up seriously the collectivization of agriculture only in the twelfth year of its power. This is precisely what Lenin called the growing over of the democratic revolution into the socialist.

"It is not the bourgeois power that grows over into a workers' and peasants' and then into a proletarian power," Trotsky wrote.

> No, the power of one class does not "grow over" from the power of another class, but is torn from it with rifle in hand.
>
> But after the working class has seized power, the democratic tasks of the proletarian regime inevitably grow over into socialist tasks. An evolutionary, organic transition to socialism is conceivable only under the *dictatorship of the proletariat*. This is Lenin's central idea.

Trotsky's primary political concern as a communist was to combat Stalin's falsification of Lenin's formula to justify subordinating the working class to bourgeois misleadership and abandoning the fight for state power. This had been Stalin's course in China toward Chiang Kai-shek's Kuomintang; it was the opposite of Lenin's conception of a workers and peasants republic arising out of a popular revolution.

Trotsky was evidently convinced, however, that the algebraic character of Lenin's formula opened it to misuse, and that the formula therefore had to be explicitly condemned in the 1933 founding program of the International Left Opposition.

That brings us to the second important aspect of the paragraph from the 1933 document.

Rejecting Lenin's formula, the paragraph expressed no concept of a transitional regime—of a dictatorship, based on an alliance of the workers and peasants, emanating from a victorious social revolution against the propertied classes, that would allow the workers to lead their toiling allies in the transition from the democratic to the socialist revolution.

If only a question of differing historical evaluations of Lenin's pre-1917 strategy were involved here, not that much time or attention would be in order. But more is involved. Among those who call themselves Trotskyists today, permanent revolution—some even spell it with a capital "P" and a capital "R"—and the confusion over the roots of our revolutionary continuity *have* reinforced tendencies toward ultraleft sectarian positions, especially on the worker-peasant alliance and on the national and colonial question.

It goes so far that a majority of those who call themselves Trotskyist are convinced that no political current is revolutionary, proletarian, and Marxist unless it understands and subscribes to Trotsky's theory of the permanent revolution. Under this mode of thought, the views cited earlier from the Cuban CP platform, from Cuban leaders Jesús Montané and Manuel Piñeiro, and from Salvadoran leader Schafik Jorge Handal, are not really Marxist at all, since none of them mention permanent revolution.

Some who call themselves Trotskyists deny the existence of a workers state in Cuba, and many have refused to recognize the existence of workers and farmers governments today in Nicaragua and Grenada. Some "third camp" currents, claiming to speak in the name of permanent revolution, refuse to recognize that the overthrow of capitalist rule, abolition of private property in the means of production, and the establishment of state property and planning in the Soviet Union, China, Yugoslavia, Albania, Vietnam, North Korea, Cuba, and the other Eastern European workers states are *conquests* of the world proletariat.

Some sectarians have made permanent revolution the test for all programs and a guide for all actions. The words, not facts and deeds, are decisive.

In fact, a substantial number of organizations that label themselves Trotskyist are hopeless, irredeemable sects. Probably 80 percent of those on a world scale who present themselves as Trotskyists—maybe it's 70 percent, maybe over 90 percent—are irreformable sectarians. The last thing that characterizes their politics is the attempt to follow Trotsky's example by applying the conquests of the Bolsheviks and the Comintern during Lenin's life and advance along the line of march laid out by the initial revolutionary communists in 1847–48.

But those hopeless sectarians are not the ones who are important to us. We're interested in the Fourth International, the international movement of which we are a part. We are interested in those who are serious revolutionists, who are carrying out a turn to the industrial working class, who can be influenced by the test of events, and who are open to political discussion.

Sectarianism and ultraleftism have been the primary, though not the only, direction in which currents in the Fourth International have erred. This has been largely the result of the historical period in which we have functioned throughout much of our existence, which left us in relative isolation from the working class and its organizations and determined our social composition. The campaign of slanders and vilification of our movement by the powerful apparatus of world Stalinism reinforced these pressures.

But I'm convinced that our movement's adherence since 1928 to Trotsky's theory of permanent revolution has also been involved. It has led us to devalue a close study and application of the strategic contributions of Bolshevism as developed in Lenin's pre-1917 writings. When we did read these materials, it was often with our minds already made up that significant aspects of them were either wrong or had been "buried by history," as Trotsky said in the Transitional Program about Lenin's formula of the revolutionary democratic dictatorship of the proletariat and peasantry. It has been a block to reading Lenin objectively, not as interpreted by others, including Trotsky.

I even think that our emphasis on the uniqueness and correctness of the theory of permanent revolution reinforced a tendency not to dig into the reports and resolutions of the first four Comintern congresses as energetically as we should have.

Of course, Trotsky would be horrified by the political positions of the big majority of those who today call themselves "Trotskyists"—a term he never used to describe our movement. His few political errors after Lenin's death which were leftist, were usually corrected as he participated in the living process of building revolutionary workers parties as part of an international movement, and as he generalized the lessons from these experiences drawing on his decade of experience as a central leader of the Soviet Communist Party and the Communist International.

Moreover, Trotsky spent a substantial amount of his time from exile in the 1930s trying to help his supporters correct serious leftist political errors on the agrarian and colonial and national questions. Let's look at several examples.

From the outset of the formation in China of groups supporting the Left Opposition in 1929, Trotsky had to combat their failure to recognize the centrality of the democratic and anti-imperialist struggles in that country. Trotsky was simultaneously polemicizing against leftist errors by the Stalin leadership of the Comintern, which by this time had responded to reverses both in its domestic and international policies by jerking its followers worldwide into a sharp "left turn." During the Comintern's so-called Third Period, it refused to recognize the evident ebb in the revolutionary struggle in China following the 1927 defeat, and downplayed the struggle for democratic demands in the name of the battle for immediate insurrection and soviet power.

Thus, for several years, Trotsky found himself writing about similar questions in patient letters to Chinese comrades and in polemics against Stalin and Stalin's supporters.

"The struggle against the military dictatorship must inevitably assume the form of *transitional revolutionary democratic demands,*" Trotsky wrote in a draft program for Chinese supporters of the Left Opposition in 1929.[68]

"The slogans of revolutionary democracy correspond best to the prerevolutionary political situation in China today," he insistently wrote them again three years later.[69] He continued:

> To arouse the workers, to organize them, to give them the possibility of relating to the national and agrarian movements in order to take the leadership of both: such is the task that falls to us. The immediate demands of the proletariat as such (length of the workday, wages, right to organize, etc.) must form the basis of our agitation.
>
> But that alone is not enough. Only these three slogans can raise the proletariat to the head of the nation: the independence of China, land to the poor peasants, the constituent assembly.

Again, in the last years of his life, Trotsky waged a political battle against a large faction in the Chinese Trotskyist movement that refused to support China, an oppressed colonial country, against the Japanese imperialist invasion and occupation—using the ultraleft argument that both sides had capitalist governments. (In 1939–40 the petty-bourgeois opposition in the SWP held this position, too, along with its refusal to defend the Soviet workers state.)

Trotsky discussed similar leftist misconceptions on the importance of the democratic and national questions with revolutionists in Indochina. When one of the first groups of Vietnamese supporters of the International Left Opposition sent Trotsky a political declaration in 1930, he wrote them a reply pointing to the serious weaknesses of the document.[70] It needed "to speak more clearly, more fully, and more precisely about the *agrarian question*," he wrote. "The *peasant question* is left out of the declaration altogether."

The declaration had condemned Vietnamese nationalism as "a reactionary ideology" that "can only forge new chains for the working class." Trotsky responded that

the nationalism of the mass of the people is the elementary form taken by their just and progressive hatred for the most skillful, capable, and ruthless of their oppressors, that is, the foreign imperialists. The proletariat does not have the right to turn its back on *this kind* of nationalism. On the contrary, it must demonstrate in practice that it is the most consistent and devoted fighter for the national liberation of Indochina.

Trotsky added that

it is very doubtful that the Indochinese workers have actually brought the national, democratic, and socialist elements of the revolution together as a single whole in their thinking as yet. . . .

We cannot arrive at the dictatorship of the proletariat by way of an a priori denial of democracy. Only by struggling for democracy can the Communist vanguard gather the majority of the oppressed nation around itself and in that way move toward the dictatorship which will also create the conditions for transition to a socialist revolution in inseparable connection with the movement of the world proletariat.

Trotsky took strong exception to a 1935 document by the South African group of the International Left Opposition, as well. They had written "that the slogan of a 'black republic' is *equally* harmful for the revolutionary cause as is the slogan of a 'South Africa for the whites.'"

Given the overwhelming majority Black population in the country, and its oppressed status, Trotsky replied:

> The South African Republic will emerge first of all as a "black" republic; this does not exclude, of course, either full equality for the whites, or brotherly relations between the two races—depending mainly on the conduct of the whites. . . .
>
> Insofar as a victorious revolution will radically change not only the relations between the classes but also between the races, and will assure to the blacks that place in the state which corresponds to their numbers, insofar will the *social* revolution in South Africa have a *national* character. . . .
>
> The proletarian revolutionaries must never forget the right of the oppressed nationalities to self-determination, including full separation, and the duty of the proletariat of the oppressing nation to defend this right with arms in hand if necessary.[71]

Faced with these types of weaknesses on the national and colonial question, Trotsky sought to make the communist approach he had learned from Lenin as clear as possible in the 1938 Transitional Program, adopted by the Socialist Workers Party in April of that year.

In the countries oppressed by imperialism, Trotsky wrote,

> the struggle for the most elementary achievements of national independence and bourgeois democracy is combined with the socialist struggle against world imperialism. Democratic slogans, transitional demands, and the problems of the socialist revolution are not divided into separate historical epochs in this struggle but stem directly from one another. . . .
>
> The central tasks of the colonial and semicolonial countries are the *agrarian revolution,* i.e., liquidation of feudal heritages, and *national independence,* i.e., the overthrow of the imperialist yoke. The two tasks are closely linked with each other.

In the colonial countries, it explains, the workers must take the leadership of the fight for national liberation. They

> must be armed with [a] democratic program. Only they will be able to summon and unite the farmers. On the basis of the revolutionary democratic program, it is necessary to oppose the workers to the "national" bourgeoisie. . . .
>
> The relative weight of the individual democratic and transitional demands in the proletariat's struggle, their mutual ties and their order of presentation, is determined by the peculiarities and specific conditions of each backward country and, to a considerable extent, by the *degree* of its backwardness. Nevertheless, the general trend of revolutionary development in all backward countries can be determined by the formula of the *permanent revolution* in the sense definitely imparted to it by the three revolutions in Russia (1905, February 1917, October 1917).

This communist strategy, then, was the *political content* that Trotsky sought to impart to the slogan permanent revolution in the founding program of the Fourth International. Trotsky's approach to the agrarian and national questions was grounded in what he had learned from Lenin, and in the positions codified in the reports and resolutions of the first four Comintern congresses, among which a large majority of the most important ones had been drafted and reported on by Lenin and Trotsky themselves.

At the same time, Trotsky's insistence on tracing the continuity of the Fourth International to his pre-1917 theory of permanent revolution, rather than Lenin's positions captured in his formula of the revolutionary democratic dictatorship of the proletariat and peasantry, reinforced rather than counterbalanced any tendency of his supporters, both in his time and in ours, to err in a sectarian direction on the peasant and national question.

That is why we say that from the standpoint of our political continuity, our Trotsky begins with his return to Russia from the United States in May 1917, not before. Trotsky, part of the Bolshevik leadership of the Soviet state, Communist Party, and the Communist International. Trotsky, along with other Bolshevik leaders fighting to continue the application of genuine communist policies in the Soviet state and the Comintern following Lenin's death. And Trotsky, after 1928, carrying on that struggle, now alone among the original Bolshevik leaders—most of whom, including Bukharin, Kamenev, Radek, Zinoviev, and Trotsky himself, will have been murdered at Stalin's orders by the end of the following decade.

Unless we approach the programmatic continuity of communism from 1847 to today in this manner, we will not succeed in explaining where Trotsky fits into it. Any other course plays into the hands of those who would seize upon Trotsky's pre-1917 views to deny his place as the continuator of genuine communism in the last seventeen years of his life. Only in this way can we learn from Trotsky the political lessons that we can reap from his writings in the 1920s and 1930s, and be able to explain their value to communists coming from different experiences and political backgrounds.

There is another problem with permanent revolution. It means very different things to different people. Once again, I put aside the hopeless sectarians, the 80 percent or so. I'm talking about what it means to some of the revolutionists who are leaders of the Fourth International.

If you read the writings of Ernest Mandel, for example, you would be led to assume that no workers and farmers government has ever existed anywhere. One definitely does not exist today in Grenada. One does not exist in Nicaragua. None ever existed in Cuba, or in Algeria. There is nothing in Mandel's published writings that says a workers and farmers government is theoretically precluded, but apparently none has ever existed. That is where his view of permanent revolution leads him on this key question of communist strategy today.[72]

Then there is Pierre Frank, a longtime leader of the Fourth

International, a communist, and a veteran of the French movement. He wrote an article in the spring 1981 issue of the French-language *Quatrième Internationale*, published by the United Secretariat of the Fourth International. The article is entitled "The Theory of Permanent Revolution."

The first sentence of that article states, "For the Fourth International, the theory of permanent revolution formulated by Leon Trotsky constitutes, to this day, the most important acquisition of revolutionary Marxism."

Think about that for a moment. The theory of permanent revolution formulated by Leon Trotsky constitutes the most important acquisition of revolutionary Marxism! Let's leave aside our fundamental theoretical acquisitions—historical materialism, the labor theory of value, and so on. Let's just consider strategic political questions. According to Pierre Frank, every strategic concept of Marx, Engels, Lenin, the Bolshevik Party, the Comintern, Trotsky himself, and anything that has been added since then—all this pales beside the theory of permanent revolution.

Comrade Frank seeks to justify this assessment by pointing to a number of countries where, as he sees it, the correctness of Trotsky's theory was demonstrated one way or another, either in victories or defeats. The stunning thing to me is that the article, which sets out to deal with this "most important acquisition" of revolutionary strategy and was finished in late 1980, does not contain one word on Nicaragua or Grenada. Not one word.

This article, moreover, was written less than a year after Pierre Frank, holding these opinions, voted against a resolution presented at the World Congress of the Fourth International that explained that the Nicaraguan government was a workers and farmers government. Evidently "the most important acquisition" of the world revolutionary movement doesn't shed much light on the most important revolutions in the Americas.

Finally, let's look at what is said about permanent revolution in a pamphlet by George Breitman, also a long-time political

leader of the Fourth International and of the Socialist Workers
Party. The pamphlet is entitled *How a Minority Can Change
Society*, and it bears rereading. It was first presented at a Mid-
west socialist conference held in Chicago in early 1964. For every error there may be in it, there are many ideas that will advance your thinking on the character of the coming American
revolution and the Afro-American struggle for national liberation.

One interesting paragraph, however, deals directly with Trotsky's theory of permanent revolution. Comrade Breitman is
briefly explaining our fundamental understanding that the
struggle for Black freedom has a dynamic that tends to go beyond the struggle for democratic rights and merge with the
struggle for socialism in this country.

"In this tendency to pass over from democratic to socialist
goals, to pass beyond the capitalist framework that now envel-
ops it," Breitman writes, the Black struggle "is similar to the
colonial struggles, which also take off from democratic aims,
such as independence and self-government, but find themselves
unable to attain those democratic aims until they wrench the
capitalist boot from off their neck."

Then he adds: "The Chinese leadership call this process 'the
uninterrupted revolution,' and Leon Trotsky called it 'the permanent revolution.'"[73]

So there's another definition. The permanent revolution is
what the Stalinists in China and their followers elsewhere meant
by uninterrupted revolution. But surely that's not right. Mao's
theory was uninterrupted revolution in a single country, as Tom
Kerry, another longtime SWP leader, once put it. Mao sought
to "revolutionize" society in order to keep a privileged caste in
power, and sacrificed the interests of the toilers of China and
the world in the process.

I could present many other examples, but just these few
should give us pause for thought. If taken back to incorporate
Trotsky's differences with Lenin before the 1917 Russian Revolution, and then brought forward to include the leftist errors

beginning in 1928 (as Pierre Frank and Ernest Mandel explicitly do), then permanent revolution leads us off the axis of our political continuity with Bolshevism and the first four congresses of the Comintern. It leads us away from the struggle for a genuinely proletarian party.

Our movement has been able to enrich our program on the basis of the experience of the world class struggle. The 1963 document adopted at the reunification congress of the Fourth International, for example, explained that guerrilla warfare "under a leadership that becomes committed to carrying the revolution through to a conclusion" had to "be consciously incorporated into the strategy of building revolutionary Marxist parties in colonial countries."[74]

Most important, we've enriched our understanding of the workers and farmers government. For a while we had agreement within the Fourth International that a workers and peasants government had come into existence in Algeria in the early 1960s.[75] But that agreement unraveled with widening political differences.

The workers and farmers government is key to our transitional program and strategy today. Without presenting to the toilers the perspective of taking governmental power, a program is simply playing at revolution. That is exactly the point raised by Comrades Piñeiro, Montané, and Handal.

A workers and farmers government is the first stage, the antechamber, of the dictatorship of the proletariat. But we know that in explaining this idea to workers, even those who think it's a good idea, they do not think of such a government in that way. The forward march of history would be much farther along if they did. And our tasks would be much easier.

We call for a workers and farmers government as a transitional slogan to raise the idea that workers, allied with other toilers, should organize to take governmental power and use it to advance their class interests. In that way, the slogan helps raise the class consciousness of the workers and cement an alliance with other exploited working people.

It is more than just a slogan, however. We believe that history has shown that in our epoch it is a workers and farmers government that will come out of a successful anticapitalist revolution. It is the first form of government following a victorious uprising against the bourgeoisie—a government that will not turn power back over to the capitalists, but will fight to take power *away* from them and use it to open up the road to deepening the mobilization of the workers and farmers and the expropriation of the exploiters.

But this is a process and it does not come with an a priori guarantee of success. In colonial and semicolonial countries, the initial tasks of the new revolutionary government are primarily those of the democratic revolution—national liberation, agrarian reform, measures to improve the conditions and expand the rights of the working class and peasantry. In the United States and other advanced capitalist countries, too, the establishment of a workers state on new property foundations will not be accomplished overnight following a victorious socialist revolution. That transition, too, will take time, organization, and class struggle, based on a governmental alliance of workers and farmers.

It is this all-important transitional stage, and the rich concreteness of the class struggle and proletarian leadership of its allies during the transition, that is lost sight of when the workers and farmers government is rejected or "jumped over."

Proletarianization and
communist continuity today

This brings us back to the starting point of this article—the political convergence of revolutionary forces, of communists originating from different experiences and heritages. The fusion of revolutionary political currents has been part of the process of developing a program and strategy for the working class from the beginning of the modern communist movement.

The Bolsheviks' fusion with Trotsky's Mezhrayonka organization in July 1917, for example, was part of forging the leadership of the Russian Revolution, and the cadre that took the lead in developing the program of the Communist International. It never crossed Lenin's mind after 1917 that Trotsky was anything but a Bolshevik, and from then on there was none better, as Lenin put it.

The Cuban Communist Party is a different party from the July 26 Movement, and a better one. Its fusion with other revolutionary forces in the 1960s to build a new party was rooted in common struggle *before* 1959 that made the triumph possible. The fusion did more than swell the new party's ranks; it enriched its outlook and breadth of class-struggle experience.

Both the Sandinista National Liberation Front and the New Jewel Movement were products of the political convergence and fusion of different currents. And a unified party that emerges from the revolution in El Salvador will be stronger politically than any one of its parts or than the current coalition.

Each time a party successfully carries out a principled fusion with other revolutionary forces, it changes and advances itself, and the end product is richer and more rounded for it. We know from our own experience over the past decade how the SWP has been changed and strengthened by fusions.

The same thing holds on the international level.

We are part of a worldwide political convergence of forces committed to making, defending, and subordinating all other considerations to extending the socialist revolution. As a result, the Fourth International today has the greatest opportunity in its history to be part of advancing the perspective it has advocated for half a century: the construction of a mass, communist International.

The leaderships of the Cuban, Nicaraguan, and Grenadian revolutions represent the revival of communism, of leaderships that practice proletarian internationalism. To paraphrase the Transitional Program, there now *are* other revolutionary currents worthy of the name, and they are playing a mighty historical role. But we must never forget that we, too, must continually show ourselves worthy of the name revolutionist.

That is where defending and building on the political conquests of the 1979 World Congress of the Fourth International becomes so important. A great deal was accomplished at that congress.

A report adopted there stressed, "that the sections of the Fourth International must make a radical *turn* to immediately organize to get a large majority of our members and leaders into industry and into industrial unions." The World Congress report pointed out that "a political radicalization of the working class—uneven and at different tempos from country to country—is on the agenda" and that "the rulers' offensive will force big changes in the industrial unions." It continued:

> The key for revolutionists is to be there, in and part of the decisive sector of the working class, prior to these showdowns.
>
> It is *there* that we will meet the forces to build the Fourth International, to build workers parties. It is *there* that we will meet the young workers, the growing numbers of women workers, the workers of oppressed nationalities, and the immigrant workers. It is inside the industrial working class that revolu-

tionary parties will get a response to our program and recruits to our movement.

The report, adopted by the Fourth International, explained:

Only parties not only proletarian in program, but in composition and experience, can lead the workers and their allies in the struggles that are on the agenda.

Only parties of industrial workers will be able to withstand the pressures, including the ideological pressures, of the ruling class. And these pressures will increase.

Only such parties will have their hand on the pulse of the working class, and thereby not misread their own attitudes, ignorance, and moods as those of the workers. In other words, only parties of industrial workers can move forward and outward.

Because the turn to industry had first been adopted by the Socialist Workers Party in 1978, was being carried out by our cadres, and we were leading the fight for this perspective in the Fourth International, I presented the report to our world movement. The report rooted the turn in the programmatic continuity of communism. "We are not blazing a new trail in this regard," the report emphasized. "In the history of the Marxist movement, the most proletarian parties have been the best parties—the most revolutionary, the least economist, the most political. Go back to the Bolsheviks. Go back to Rosa Luxemburg. Go back to the goals the Fourth International set for itself, with the advice and leadership of Trotsky, at the end of the 1930s."[76]

A resolution presenting a communist perspective for the fight for women's emancipation was adopted at the 1979 World Congress. It was based on the programmatic foundations laid by Marx and Engels and by the Communist International. Challenges by bourgeois and petty-bourgeois feminists to our materialist understanding of the origins of women's oppression were addressed and rejected by the World Congress resolution.[77]

A critical balance sheet was drawn concerning the ultraleft disorientation of the Fourth International that had begun in the late 1960s around a disastrous continental strategic line for Latin America. As a result of this erroneous line, the 1979 World Congress recognized, "many of the cadres and parties of the Fourth International were politically disarmed in the face of the widespread, but false idea that a small group of courageous and capable revolutionaries could set in motion a process leading to a socialist revolution. The process of rooting our parties in the working class and oppressed masses was hindered."

In addition, there were debates at the 1979 World Congress foreshadowing the big challenges facing the Fourth International today. There were sharp differences, for example, over the evaluation of the deepening revolution in Nicaragua. A majority of delegates rejected the assessment in the resolution supported by delegates from the SWP that a workers and farmers government had been established in Nicaragua, and that the Cuban and Nicaraguan leaderships were proletarian revolutionists.

A related debate also opened there around counterposed resolutions on the dictatorship of the proletariat. The importance of the issues at the center of that debate has emerged more and more clearly as the discussion advances in the Fourth International today over what is the revolutionary continuity of communism and how that relates to the responsibilities and opportunities posed by the emergence of Marxist leaderships in Central America and the Caribbean and by the deepening polarization and working-class politicalization in the United States and other imperialist countries.[78]

Should the Fourth International not rise to the challenge of becoming part of the process of political convergence that is under way today, then the conquests of the 1979 World Congress will unravel at an accelerating pace, and the errors made there will be deepened and extended rather than corrected. In this case, the Fourth International as a whole will not move for-

ward in the construction of parties made up in their big majority of industrial workers, parties that are increasingly multina-
tional in membership and leadership, that have their eyes on
the young workers and the most oppressed and exploited layers of the working class and its allies. A retreat would also set in
from the communist course toward the struggle for women's
rights. Positions long taken for granted—unconditional political defense of the workers states against imperialism; the anti-
imperialist united front in the oppressed nations—would begin to erode.

If the Fourth International does rise to these challenges, however, it can bring an irreplaceable contribution to the process of
political convergence. Along with the communist continuity we
hold in common with other revolutionists today—going back
to Marx, Engels, Lenin, the Bolshevik Party, and the early Comintern—we are communists who bring something else into the
convergence. We are communists who bring a rich understanding of the resistance in the Soviet Communist Party leadership
during the 1920s to the retreat by the developing bureaucratic
caste away from proletarian internationalism and a revolutionary proletarian strategy.

We bring to the communist movement a rich understanding of Trotsky's political and strategic contributions during his
last exile. This includes not only his defense of the Comintern
program, but his application of it to new political developments
in the 1930s. Trotsky sounded the alarm at the rise of fascism
in Germany and across Europe, analyzing it scientifically, and
tirelessly agitating for the communist and social-democratic
parties and the trade unions each of those parties led to forge a
united front to defeat reaction in the streets. He exposed the Stalinists' class-collaborationist Popular Front course, which led to
the devastating defeat of revolutionary openings in France and
Spain by subordinating the struggles of workers and farmers
to the class needs of the "democratic" wing of the bourgeoisie.
He analyzed the consequences of the bloody consolidation by
the privileged bureaucratic caste of its political monopoly in the

Soviet Union and the intimately related Stalinist degeneration of the Comintern.

At the close of the 1930s, Trotsky initiated and—on a world scale—politically fought for the effort directed in this country by James P. Cannon and other SWP leaders to advance the proletarianization of the party by leading the cadres deeper into the unions and mass workers movements. As the experience of the Bolsheviks had shown a quarter century earlier, that course was essential to prepare a communist party and its cadres for the enormous pressures that would accompany the imperialist war, a war that by then had become inevitable.

To bring these contributions to the world movement, however, we must be able to face up to the test of experience from the revolutionary class struggle since World War II. We must recognize that Trotsky's theory of permanent revolution is *not* a correct generalization of the historic program and strategy of communism. In comparison to the reports and resolutions of the early Comintern, which were rooted in the pre-1917 program and strategy of Bolshevism, permanent revolution weakens rather than enriches our understanding of the worker-farmer alliance, and of the relationship and the transition between the democratic and socialist revolution in the nations oppressed by imperialism. Throughout most of our history, our adherence to permanent revolution has led us to pay insufficient attention to reconquering our political continuity with the documents of the Comintern and with Lenin's pre-1917 political writings. It has left us with an incomplete and one-sided understanding of the political preparations for the Russian Revolution and the roots of the Comintern, depriving us of some rich lessons.

That is what we in the Socialist Workers Party have discovered over the past five years since we made our turn to industry, since we began becoming more proletarian, since we began to emerge from the semisectarian existence imposed on us by conditions in the 1950s and 1960s, and since we began following more closely the course of the revolutions and proletarian leaderships in Central America and the Caribbean.

Our deepening integration into the working class and labor movement of this country first led us back to Marx and Engels. That began in 1978 when we began the turn to industry and, at the same time, organized to launch a leadership school. The school from its first session has been structured around an intensive reading and study of the political writings of Marx and Engels—their evolution into scientific communists in the 1840s; their participation in the founding of the first communist organization of the modern working class in 1847–48, and in drafting its political program and its rules; their participation as proletarian leaders of the democratic revolution in Germany in 1848 and the conclusions they drew from that and the other 1848 revolutions; their role in founding the First International and defending its programmatic and organizational foundations against anarchists and petty-bourgeois currents of all stripes; the conclusions they drew from the Paris Commune; their extensive observations and analyses of the Civil War and class struggle in the United States; and more.

Then, as the revolutions in the Americas advanced, as we became more of a party *of* the working class in this country, and as our understanding of our heritage in Marx and Engels grew, we launched an intensive reading and study of Lenin's political writings in every branch of the SWP.[79]

And we discovered a Lenin and a political continuity we had not known.

These have been strengths of the Socialist Workers Party over the past several years. We responded to the deepening crisis of capitalism and the politicalization of the working class by taking bold steps to change the axis of our work and our social composition, to become a party that in its membership and leadership has more young workers, more workers who are Black, more workers whose first language is Spanish.

We recognized and embraced the emergence of proletarian leaderships of socialist revolutions in this hemisphere and placed defense of those revolutions at the center of our political activity.

We have not been afraid to learn from the actual unfolding

of the class struggle in this country and worldwide, to learn from other revolutionists. We have not been afraid to approach questions objectively and critically, including our own heritage and in doing so we are strengthening that heritage.

In some ways, the shift I am proposing is one of the biggest changes in our movement since we first emerged, more than half a century ago, as a distinct political current in world politics. Since that time, permanent revolution in all its meanings has been a guiding concept of our entire world movement, including the SWP.

In an even more important way, however, this is not such a big change. It is no change whatsoever from the line of march charted by the first scientific communists in 1847–48, and followed by Marx and Engels from that time until their deaths. No change from the program and strategy of Bolshevism that, beginning in 1903, laid the foundation for the victory fourteen years later of the first socialist revolution, the proletariat's first experience with its class dictatorship. No change from the course charted by the Communist International in Lenin's time between 1919 and 1923.

And it is no change from the political struggle by Trotsky from the mid-1920s through the 1930s to preserve, build on, and apply this communist continuity against the efforts of a privileged bureaucratic layer in the USSR to throw out proletarian internationalism, to abandon the struggle to extend the world socialist revolution. In fact, in the 1980s it is *only* by recognizing that permanent revolution is wrong as a generalization of the communist program and strategy that we can rediscover Trotsky more richly and more accurately as the continuator of the battle of the world working class that reached its highest point with the victory of the Russian Revolution, and that has won new victories since then.

All revolutionists today have a great deal to learn from Trotsky, who was one of the great Marxists of this century and helped pass on to us what our class learned from Marx, Engels, and Lenin. But, our movement must change the way we have used and explained Trotsky's contributions.

When we read Trotsky's writings today—after Cuba, Nicaragua, and Grenada, after beginning to live through the politicalization of the working class in this country—we will find them more useful and gain new insights. If this were not true, we would not be approaching our continuity as a living program. Because we don't only take *from* our program, we also take *to* it. We are continually building and rebuilding continuity, enriching and critically changing our understanding of that continuity, and applying it to new situations.

Our political continuity is the program and strategy of communism from the days of Marx and Engels, through the forging of the Bolshevik Party by Lenin, through the 1917 revolution in Russia, through the formation of the Communist International and the fight to preserve it, through the founding documents of the Fourth International and subsequent additions to them.

Along with Lenin's works, the best place to discover that continuity is in the documents of the first four Comintern congresses.[80] When we read and study those documents, we are absorbing the political course that made possible the conquest of power by the workers and peasants of Russia under Bolshevik leadership. Because the Comintern program incorporates and builds on the program and strategy captured in Lenin's formula of the revolutionary democratic dictatorship of the proletariat and peasantry.

Our movement today needs to read, study, and absorb the richness of the Communist International's resolutions, reports, and debates. These documents will help prepare us for what lies ahead in the class struggle in this country and around the world. This is all the more important, because this is exactly what other revolutionists are going back to in order to find answers. We share this in common with them.

We will read the Comintern documents not through "permanent revolution" eyes, but with our eyes on what's happening in the world class struggle today. We will read Lenin not through Trotsky's eyes, but with our own eyes and based on our own experiences, exactly as Trotsky did. In doing so we will be able to find in Trotsky the richest political writings, and the best application of the communist program and strategy, of any Marxist between 1923 and 1940. And we will bring this to other revolutionists.

As we read Trotsky with a fuller knowledge of Marx, Engels, and Lenin, we will gain even more insight from his writings. We will be more capable of applying those lessons to the developments unfolding today in the class struggle in this country and internationally.

If you read Lenin's political writings you find that they are filled with quotations, references, and paraphrases from the writings of Marx and Engels. Throughout a third of a century in the revolutionary working-class movement, Lenin did not exhaust the political lessons he could learn from Marx and Engels. When Trotsky was assassinated in 1940, he had not exhausted the lessons he could learn from Marx, Engels, and Lenin. And we can be sure, no matter how ripe an age we grow to in the working-class struggle, that none of us will exhaust the lessons we can learn from Marx, Engels, Lenin, and Trotsky.

If we approach our revolutionary continuity in this way, then Trotsky's contributions will find their place in the political arsenal of the international communist movement as the world revolution progresses.

Of course, none of this will happen overnight. What we are living through today is an international *political* convergence of communists, one that has no common organizational framework and no immediate prospects for one. How quickly that will change, and the forms it might take, will be determined by big class forces and developments in world politics that are beyond our immediate control or that of any revolutionary current. In this, as in everything we do, objectivity, a sense of being part of living history, and even a little patience combined with a sense of proportion are good qualities for communists.

Cuban Communist Party leader Carlos Rafael Rodríguez demonstrates all three of these qualities in a perceptive passage in the 1970 article "Lenin and the Colonial Question."

After summarizing Lenin's report and theses on the national and colonial question adopted at the second Comintern congress, Rodríguez poses the question:

"What has been the test of history?

"It is not possible for us to go into a systematic examination of how Lenin's theses have been applied to the reality of the colonial and semicolonial movements," he answers.

> Not only would that be beyond the scope of this study—whose principal aim is exposition—but also, the circumstances themselves make this undesirable. This is because the first question posed would be, "To what degree were Lenin's theses really put into practice?" That question would lead us to examine fully the whole policy of the Communist International and its sections during a lengthy historical period. To do so in the conditions of discord still prevailing in the international Communist movement would be impossible.

Rodríguez does have patience and a sense of history. He is confident that as times change, so will what can and must be said. Referring back to the question, "To what degree were Lenin's theses really put into practice?" he continues:

> It is indispensable to at least register the fact that the problem exists. The time will come when it will not only be possible but necessary to take it up in depth. The fact that Trotsky's and Zinoviev's struggles against J. V. Stalin's policy in China in 1926–27 stand at the center of the problem does not give one the excuse of peremptorily declaring, a priori, that the solution lies in a simple apologia for the official decisions of the Comintern.

Rodríguez's unanswered question, in fact, is what Salvadoran CP leader Schafik Jorge Handal begins to address in the article we've discussed earlier. It is a question the Cuban leaders continue to speak to by helping to draw and generalize the lessons from their own experiences and those of the toilers throughout the Caribbean and Central and South America.

We in the SWP can and should express our conclusions today on these questions. And we can be confident that when, to paraphrase Rodríguez, the time comes when it will not only be possible but necessary for the entire revolutionary communist movement to take up these questions in depth, we will have a contribution to make that other revolutionists will listen to and consider, as we will do with theirs. *Our* Trotsky—the continuator of Lenin's course, the proletarian communist—will find his place.

While there are many things about the outcome of the current political convergence of revolutionists that we have no way of knowing in advance, there is one thing I think we can say is likely—*communism* will be the common name of the international workers organization that develops out of this process now under way. That will be the name of the revolutionary workers parties that will be formed and of the international leadership organization they forge.

This will be true for the same reason that Marx and Engels took that name.

For the same reason that the Bolsheviks in 1918 changed the name of their party from the Russian Social Democratic Labor Party to the Communist Party.

And for the same reason the new revolutionary International was given that name in 1919. The Bolsheviks could certainly have gotten away with suggesting that it be called the Bolshevik International. That would have been greeted with the hurrahs of advanced workers throughout the world. If there were ever heroes of the oppressed and exploited of the world, it was the Bolsheviks in those years—revolutionists who had done the job, who took power, and set out to help toilers everywhere do the same.

But the Bolsheviks said no, the correct word is *communist*. As Lenin had explained earlier in motivating the adoption of that name for the Bolshevik Party, the word *socialist* wouldn't do the trick. Socialist *is* the right description of the revolution against capitalist rule, as well as of the new society that the dictatorship of the proletariat will initially make possible on a world scale. Basing himself on Marx and Engels, Lenin explained that this new socialist world order will be based on state ownership of the means of production, and that the wealth produced by society collectively will be distributed "according to the amount of work performed by each individual."

However, Lenin continued, "Our Party looks farther ahead: socialism must inevitably evolve gradually into communism." A communist society, with its abundance and highly developed productive capacity, could then distribute its wealth on the basis of the principles, "From each according to his ability, to each according to his needs."[81]

That is why Marx and Engels chose the name *Manifesto of the Communist Party* for the proletariat's first document generalizing its line of march over the entire historical epoch of its struggle to become dominant in the world, thus laying the basis for the abolition of all classes and forms of exploitation and oppression.

In 1914, the Second International, which for a quarter century embodied the continuity of Marxism, betrayed that heritage. The decision to call its successor *communist*, therefore, meant not only going back to a name, but also picking up a thread that could tie the new Third International most strongly to its real continuity.

The July 26 Movement, too, could have argued to keep some name connected with its particular Cuban origins and history. But leaders of the Cuban Revolution chose not to. After several years of discussion, they proposed the name Communist Party, and that was what was adopted in 1965.

Communism. That is the common heritage that every revolutionist, coming from every point of view, will find of value as we move forward and move closer.

Most of us will not call our movement "Trotskyist" before this decade is out, just as Trotsky never did. We in the Socialist

Workers Party, like Trotsky, are communists.

Of course, this change in what we are called and call ourselves will only occur if there is revolutionary progress in the international class struggle. Without advances of the international working-class revolution, without convergence and fusions, then each current is stuck with whatever other people see them as, based on whatever their origins are. There's no use in griping about it. That's just the way it will be.

But that is not what is happening in the world now. What is happening is an overall rise in the international class struggle, with its center being the extension of the socialist revolution in Central America and the Caribbean.

Many still use the name communist today who don't deserve it. But that, too, will change as the revolutionary workers step forward and pose an alternative leadership. Those workers will reclaim that name.

The international working class, as Trotsky was confident it would, has made new conquests and is fighting to come to the leadership of the battle for national liberation, women's emancipation, democratic rights, and against imperialist war. As we learned from Trotsky, defending every advance of the toilers, no matter how small, every advance of the struggle for national liberation, together with the unconditional defense of the conquests of the Russian Revolution and of every subsequent workers state is vital to the extension of the world socialist revolution and to the regeneration of communism.

Along with other fighters in our class worldwide, we in the Socialist Workers Party are reconquering and enriching our understanding of the political continuity of communism. We are finding ways to explain to other workers in this country why our class needs a workers and farmers government, and we are using the examples of Cuba, Nicaragua, and Grenada to show what working people can accomplish when we conquer political power.

It is along this road that we will build a centralized, proletarian communist party in this country. It is along this road that we will take part in the rebirth of a genuine communist movement worldwide. And it is along this road that our class here in the United States will join, as selfless militants, in an unfolding American socialist revolution.

Notes

Some of the page references cited below for Pathfinder Press titles may not correspond to the printing you have. Since 1998 an international team of some 150 volunteers has been working to digitize all Pathfinder titles so the publisher can take advantage of new printing processes to produce books more economically. In the course of this work, the type size of many books and pamphlets has been increased to make them more readable, and most works have been reformatted, thus changing the pagination.

1. James P. Cannon, *The History of American Trotskyism, 1928–38: Report of a Participant* (New York: Pathfinder Press, 2002).

2. *Programmatic Platform of the Communist Party of Cuba* (Havana: Department of Revolutionary Orientation of the Central Committee of the Communist Party of Cuba, 1976), pp. 46–57.

3. Jesús Montané, "Speech by Cuban Leader Jesús Montané," *Intercontinental Press* (January 31, 1983), pp. 58–61.

4. Manuel Piñeiro, "Three Keys to Revolutionary Victory," *Intercontinental Press* (January 31, 1983), pp. 62–64.

5. For a discussion of the first three Comintern congresses by longtime SWP leader Farrell Dobbs, see Dobbs, *Revolutionary Continuity: Birth of the Communist Movement, 1918–1922* (New York: Pathfinder Press, 1983).

6. Schafik Jorge Handal, "Salvadoran FMLN Leader Discusses Strategy for Latin American Revolution," *Intercontinental Press* (November 15, 1982), pp. 819–24.

7. "The Organizational Structure of the Communist Parties, the Methods and Content of Their Work," in *Theses, Resolutions and Manifestos of the First Four Congresses of the Third International* (London: Ink Links, 1980), p. 259.

8. Karl Marx and Frederick Engels, *Collected Works* (New York: In-

ternational Publishers, 1976), vol. 6, p. 504.

9. Karl Marx and Frederick Engels, *Collected Works*, vol. 23, p. 175.

10. *Founding the Communist International: Proceedings and Documents of the First Congress, March 1919* (New York: Pathfinder, 1987), p. 243.

11. Leon Trotsky, "The Death Agony of Capitalism and the Tasks of the Fourth International" in *The Transitional Program for Socialist Revolution* (New York: Pathfinder Press, 1977), p. 165. The Transitional Program was first adopted by the Socialist Workers Party in 1938. See *The Founding of the Socialist Workers Party: Minutes and Resolutions, 1938–39* (New York: Pathfinder, 1982).

12. Carlos Rafael Rodríguez, *Lenin and the Colonial Question*, in *New International*, vol. 1 (New York, 1983).

13. Frederick Engels, "The Communists and Karl Heinzen," in Karl Marx and Frederick Engels, *Collected Works*, vol. 6, pp. 303–4.

14. "Manifesto of the Communist Party," in Marx and Engels *Collected Works*, vol. 6, p. 497.

15. Karl Marx and Frederick Engels, "Marx to Joseph Weydemeyer," in *Collected Works*, vol. 39, pp. 62–64.

16. Leon Trotsky, *The First Five Years of the Communist International* (New York: Pathfinder Press, 1972), vol. 1, p. 122.

17. V.I. Lenin, "Report of the Commission on the National and the Colonial Questions," in *Collected Works* (Moscow: Progress Publishers, 1974), vol. 31, p. 244.

18. V.I. Lenin, "Report on the International Situation and the Fundamental Tasks of the Communist International," in *Collected Works*, vol. 31, p. 232.

19. *Workers of the World and Oppressed Peoples, Unite!* (New York: Pathfinder, 1991), vol. 2, p. 696.

20. Lenin, "Report on the Tactics of the Russian Communist Party," in *Collected Works*, vol. 32, p. 482.

21. Lenin, "'Left-Wing' Communism—An Infantile Disorder," in *Collected Works*, vol. 31, pp. 21–22.

22. Lenin, "New Times and Old Mistakes in a New Guise," in *Collected Works*, vol. 33, p. 28.

23. Leon Trotsky, "Manifesto on China of the International Left Opposition," in *Leon Trotsky on China* (New York: Pathfinder Press, 1976), p. 528.

24. "The Platform of the Opposition," in Leon Trotsky, *The Challenge*

of the Left Opposition (1926–27) (New York: Pathfinder Press, 1980), pp. 368–73.

25. Leon Trotsky, "Class Relations in the Chinese Revolution," in *Leon Trotsky on China,* pp. 156–57. Another 1927 article by Trotsky—entitled "What Were My Disagreements with Lenin on the Character of the Russian Revolution"—was translated and run in issue no. 5 of *New International* (New York, 1985).

26. Leon Trotsky, *The Third International After Lenin* (New York: Pathfinder Press, 1996), p. 142.

27. Leon Trotsky, *The Permanent Revolution and Results and Prospects* (New York: Pathfinder Press, 1969); Leon Trotsky, *1905* (New York: Vintage Books, 1972).

28. *Results and Prospects,* pp. 69, 122.

29. V.I. Lenin, "The Aim of the Proletarian Struggle in Our Revolution," in Lenin, *Collected Works,* vol. 15, pp. 360–79.

30. V.I. Lenin, "The Third International and Its Place in History," in Lenin, *Collected Works,* vol. 29, p. 310.

31. Leon Trotsky, "The Social Forces in the Russian Revolution," in *Lenin's Struggle for a Revolutionary International* (New York: Pathfinder Press, 1984), pp. 515–21.

32. V.I. Lenin, "On the Two Lines in the Revolution," in Lenin, *Collected Works,* vol. 21, p. 420.

33. Lenin, *Collected Works,* vol. 9, pp. 17–140.

34. Leon Trotsky, "Speech to the Seventh (Enlarged) Plenum of the ECCI," in Trotsky, *The Challenge of the Left Opposition (1926–27),* pp. 176–79.

35. Isaac Deutscher, *The Prophet Armed* (New York: Vintage Books, 1965), p. 217.

36. Leon Trotsky, "Open Letter to the Editorial Board of *Kommunist,*" in *Lenin's Struggle for a Revolutionary International* (New York: Pathfinder Press, 1984), pp. 235–38.

37. Lenin, "The War and Russian Social Democracy," in *Collected Works,* vol. 21, pp. 32–33.

38. The political battle over a proletarian internationalist course during World War I is fully documented in Pathfinder's *Lenin's Struggle for a Revolutionary International,* cited above. The collection includes articles and speeches by Lenin, Trotsky, and other leaders of the revolutionary, centrist, and social-patriotic wings of the international workers movement, as well as documents of the Zimmerwald Left.

39. V.I. Lenin, "The Irish Rebellion of 1916," and Leon Trotsky, "Lessons of the Events in Dublin," in *New International*, no. 1 (New York, 1983). The article by Lenin can also be found in *Collected Works*, vol. 22, pp. 353–58. Both the Lenin and Trotsky articles on the Easter uprising are in *Lenin's Struggle for a Revolutionary International*.

40. Leon Trotsky, "The Lessons of the Great Year," in Trotsky, *Our Revolution* (New York: Henry Holt & Co., 1918), pp. 176–77.

41. Leon Trotsky, *The Challenge of the Left Opposition (1923–25)* (New York: Pathfinder Press, 1975), p. 263.

42. Trotsky, *The Challenge of the Left Opposition (1926–27)*, p. 372.

43. Trotsky, "The Chinese revolution and the Theses of Comrade Stalin," in *Leon Trotsky on China*, p. 178.

44. Leon Trotsky, "Summary and Perspectives of the Chinese Revolution," in Trotsky, *The Third International After Lenin*, pp. 180–240. Also in *Leon Trotsky on China*, pp. 320–76.

45. Leon Trotsky, "Report on the Fourth World Congress," in *The First Five Years of the Communist International*, (New York: Pathfinder Press, 1972), vol. 2, p. 324.

46. Leon Trotsky, "Theses on the Economic Situation of Soviet Russia from the Standpoint of the Socialist Revolution," in *The First Five Years of the Communist International*, vol. 2, p. 269.

47. Leon Trotsky, "Is the Time Ripe for the Slogan: 'The United States of Europe'?" in *The First Five Years of the Communist International*, vol. 2, p. 345.

48. Fidel Castro, *Fidel Castro Speeches: Cuba's Internationalist Foreign Policy* (New York: Pathfinder Press, 1981), p. 11.

49. Jean Van Heijenoort, *With Trotsky in Exile* (Cambridge: Harvard University Press, 1978).

50. Leon Trotsky, "Declaration of the Bolshevik-Leninist Delegation at the Conference of Left Socialist and Communist Organizations," in *Writings of Leon Trotsky, 1933–34* (New York: Pathfinder Press, 1975), p. 40.

51. "Imperialist War and the Proletarian World Revolution," in *Documents of the Fourth International, 1933–40* (New York: Pathfinder Press, 1973), p. 327.

52. Leon Trotsky, "The USSR in War," in *In Defense of Marxism* (New York: Pathfinder Press, 1995), p. 64.

53. "The Colonial World and the Second Imperialist War," in *Documents of the Fourth International*, p. 391.

54. Leon Trotsky, "Closer to the Proletarians of the 'Colored' Races!" in *Writings of Leon Trotsky, 1932* (New York: Pathfinder Press, 1973), p. 131.

55. Leon Trotsky, *Writings of Leon Trotsky, 1937–38* (New York: Pathfinder Press, 1976), p. 27.

56. Leon Trotsky, *Leon Trotsky on Black Nationalism and Self-Determination* (New York: Pathfinder Press, 1978).

57. Van Heijenoort, *With Trotsky in Exile*, p. 130.

58. Trotsky, *The Transitional Program*, p. 184.

59. Van Heijenoort, *With Trotsky in Exile*, p. 149.

60. Leon Trotsky, *Writings of Leon Trotsky, 1939–40* (New York: Pathfinder Press, 1973), pp. 63–84.

61. Trotsky, *The Permanent Revolution*, p. 172.

62. Trotsky, *Leon Trotsky on China*, pp. 640–54.

63. See Jack Barnes, *For a Workers and Farmers Government in the United States* (New York: Pathfinder Press, 1985) as well as his related article in issue no. 4 of *New International*.

64. Leon Trotsky, "The Death Agony of Capitalism and the Tasks of the Fourth International," in Trotsky, *The Transitional Program for Socialist Revolution*, pp. 135–85.

65. Jack Barnes, *For a Workers and Farmers Government in the United States*, p. 5. See also Joseph Hansen, *The Workers and Farmers Government* (New York: Pathfinder Press, 1974).

66. "The International Left Opposition, Its Tasks and Methods," in *Documents of the Fourth International*, p. 24.

67. Leon Trotsky, "The Spanish Revolution and the Dangers Threatening It," in Trotsky, *The Spanish Revolution (1931–39)* (New York: Pathfinder Press, 1973), pp. 125–49.

68. Trotsky, "The Political Situation in China and the Tasks of the Bolshevik-Leninist Opposition," in *Leon Trotsky on China*, p. 448.

69. Trotsky, "For a Strategy of Action, Not Speculation," in *Leon Trotsky on China*, p. 591.

70. Leon Trotsky, "On the Declaration of the Indochinese Oppositionists," in *Writings of Leon Trotsky, 1930–31* (New York: Pathfinder Press, 1973), pp. 29–33.

71. Leon Trotsky, "On the South African Theses," in *Writings of Leon Trotsky, 1934–35* (New York: Pathfinder Press, 1974), pp. 335–43. See also Leon Trotsky, *The Transitional Program for Socialist Revolution*, pp. 72–73.

72. For a more complete presentation of the political and theoretical questions raised by Mandel in this regard, see Doug Jenness, *Ernest Mandel, Bolshevism and the Russian Revolution: A Debate* (New York: Pathfinder, 1985).

73. George Breitman, *How a Minority Can Change Society* (New York: Pathfinder Press, 1971), p. 25.

74. *Dynamics of World Revolution Today* (New York: Pathfinder Press, 1974), p. 19.

75. See Hansen, *The Workers and Farmers Government.*

76. Jack Barnes, "The Turn and Building a World Communist Movement," in Jack Barnes, *The Changing Face of U.S. Politics* (New York: Pathfinder Press, 1994), pp. 211–31.

77. The resolution "Socialist Revolution and the Struggle for Women's Liberation" is published in *Women's Liberation and the Line of March of the Working Class: Part I* (New York: Pathfinder, 1992). The resolution had been previously adopted by the August 1979 convention of the Socialist Workers Party. The report on the resolution by Mary-Alice Waters adopted by that convention is included in the above Pathfinder collection. Waters was also the reporter on the resolution at the World Congress later that year.

78. The report and resolution on Nicaragua submitted by the Socialist Workers Party to the 1979 World Congress are published in issue no. 9 of *New International,* pp. 57–116. Other reports and resolutions from that congress can be found in *1979 World Congress of the Fourth International* (New York: Pathfinder Press, 1980).

79. Copies of the Lenin study guides are available in *Two Study Guides on Lenin's Writings* (New York: Pathfinder, 1988).

80. In addition to the titles already cited, one of the best single sources is V.I. Lenin, *Speeches at Congresses of the Communist International,* (Moscow: Progress Publishers, 1972). Also, since this talk was given in 1982, Pathfinder has published six volumes under the series title "The Communist International in Lenin's Time," including the documents of the first two congresses of the Communist International, which are in *Founding the Communist International* and the two-volume *Workers of the World and Oppressed Peoples, Unite!*

81. Lenin, "The Tasks of the Proletariat in Our Revolution," in *Collected Works,* vol. 24, pp. 84–85.

Index

The Changing Face of U.S. Politics

WORKING-CLASS POLITICS AND THE TRADE UNIONS
Jack Barnes

Building the kind of party the working class needs to prepare for coming class battles—battles through which they will revolutionize themselves, their unions, and all of society. It is a handbook for workers, farmers, and youth repelled by the class inequalities, economic instability, racism, women's oppression, cop violence, and wars endemic to capitalism, and who are seeking the road toward effective action to overturn that exploitative system and join in reconstructing the world on new, socialist foundations. Also in French and Spanish. $23

The History of American Trotskyism, 1928-38

REPORT OF A PARTICIPANT
James P. Cannon

In twelve talks given in 1942, Cannon recounts the early efforts by communists in the U.S. to emulate the Bolsheviks and build a new kind of proletarian party. Concentrating on the years 1928-38, he carries the story from the first steps forward by vanguard workers politically responding to the victory of the October 1917 Russian Revolution up to the eve of World War II, when the communist organization in the U.S. takes the name Socialist Workers Party. With a new preface by Jack Barnes. Also in French and Spanish. $22.

Capitalism's World Disorder

Working-class Politics at the Millennium
JACK BARNES

The social devastation and financial panic, the coarsening of politics, the cop brutality and acts of imperialist aggression accelerating around us—all are the product not of something gone wrong but of the lawful workings of capitalism. Yet the future can be changed by the united struggle and selfless action of workers and farmers conscious of their power to transform the world. $23.95

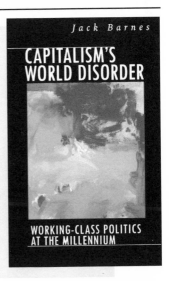

Cuba and the Coming American Revolution

JACK BARNES

"There will be a victorious revolution in the United States before there will be a victorious counterrevolution in Cuba." That statement, made by Fidel Castro in 1961, remains as accurate today as when it was spoken. This is a book about the class struggle in the United States, where the revolutionary capacities of workers and farmers are today as utterly discounted by the ruling powers as were those of the Cuban toilers. And just as wrongly. It is about the example set by the people of Cuba that revolution is not only necessary—it can be made. $13.00

The Communist Manifesto

KARL MARX AND FREDERICK ENGELS

Founding document of the modern working-class movement, published in 1848. Explains why communism is derived not from preconceived principles but from *facts* and from proletarian movements springing from the actual class struggle. $3.95

State AND Revolution

State and Revolution
V. I. Lenin
On the eve of the October 1917 Russian revolution, Lenin reaffirms the views of Marx and Engels—and lessons from the 1905 and February 1917 revolutions—on the need for workers to establish their own government and state. $5.00

For a Workers and Farmers Government in the United States
Jack Barnes
Explains why the workers and farmers government is "the most powerful instrument the working class can wield" as it moves toward expropriating the capitalists and landlords and opening the road to socialism. 8½ x 11 format. $7.00

The Workers and Farmers Government
Joseph Hansen
How experiences in revolutions following World War II in Yugoslavia, China, Algeria, and Cuba enriched communists' theoretical understanding of revolutionary governments of the toilers. 8½ x 11 format. $7.00

Two Study Guides on Lenin's Writings
Guides to the study of Lenin's political writings. The first series centers on the Bolsheviks' conception of the class forces and political strategy for the Russian revolution (1902-1917). The second, drawing on writings following the October 1917 victory, focuses on strengthening the worker-peasant base of soviet power and launching the Communist International. $3.00

Communism and the Fight for a Popular Revolutionary Government: 1848 to Today
(in New International no. 3)
Mary-Alice Waters
Traces the continuity in the fight by the working-class movement over 150 years to wrest political power from the small minority of wealthy property owners, whose class rule, Waters says, is inseparably linked to the "misery, hunger, and disease of the great majority of humanity." Also includes "'A Nose for Power': Preparing the Nicaraguan Revolution" by Tomás Borge. $8.00

FROM PATHFINDER. SEE FRONT OF BOOK FOR ADDRESSES.

The Cuban Revolution

To Speak the Truth
*Why Washington's 'Cold War' against
Cuba Doesn't End*
Fidel Castro and Che Guevara
In historic speeches before the United
Nations and UN bodies, Guevara and
Castro address the workers of the world,
explaining why the U.S. government so
hates the example set by the socialist
revolution in Cuba and why
Washington's efforts to destroy it will
fail. $16.95

Che Guevara Talks
to Young People
"If this revolution is Marxist, it is because it
discovered by its own methods the road pointed out
by Marx." Ernesto Che Guevara, 1960. Eight
speeches from 1959 to 1964 by the legendary
Argentine-born leader of the Cuban Revolution.
Preface by Armando Hart, introduction by Mary-
Alice Waters. $14.95

Playa Girón/Bay of Pigs
*Washington's First Military Defeat
in the Americas*
Fidel Castro, José Ramón Fernández
In less than 72 hours of combat in April 1961,
Cuba's revolutionary armed forces defeated an
invasion by 1,500 mercenaries organized by
Washington. In the process, the Cuban people set
an example for workers, farmers, and youth
throughout the world that with political
consciousness, class solidarity, unflinching
courage, and revolutionary leadership, it is
possible to stand up to enormous might and
seemingly insurmountable odds—and win. $20.00

DYNAMICS OF THE CUBAN REVOLUTION
by Joseph Hansen

How did the Cuban
revolution come about? Why
does it represent, as Joseph
Hansen put it, an "unbearable
challenge" to U.S. imperialism?
What political challenges has it
confronted? This compilation,
written with polemical clarity
as the revolution advanced, is
irreplaceable in understanding
the Cuban revolution today.
$22.95

JAMES P. CANNON: THE INTERNATIONALIST
by Joseph Hansen

If a revolutionist in the United States tried to dictate program
and tactics to those in another country, writes Joseph Hansen,
then pioneer American communist James P. Cannon would
have done "his utmost to squelch such presumption on the
grounds that it did not evince an internationalist attitude but
just the contrary." The first duty of a proletarian
internationalist in the U.S. is "to become absorbed in the
problems of the American revolution." $6.00

FROM PATHFINDER. SEE FRONT OF BOOK FOR ADDRESSES.

REVOLUTIONARY CONTINUITY

Marxist Leadership in the United States

Dobbs explains how successive generations of fighters took part in the struggles of the U.S. labor movement, seeking to build a leadership that could advance the class interests of workers and small farmers and link up with fellow toilers around the world.

THE EARLY YEARS, 1848-1917
$17.95

BIRTH OF THE COMMUNIST MOVEMENT, 1918-1922
$18.95

Malcolm X Talks to Young People

"I for one will join in with anyone, I don't care what color you are, as long as you want to change this miserable condition that exists on this earth."
— Malcolm X, December 1964. Also includes his 1965 interview with the *Young Socialist* magazine. $10.95

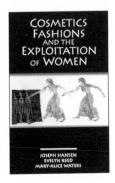

Cosmetics, Fashions, and the Exploitation of Women

JOSEPH HANSEN, EVELYN REED, AND MARY-ALICE WATERS

How big business plays on women's second-class status and social insecurities to market cosmetics and rake in profits. The introduction by Waters explains how the entry of millions of women into the workforce during and after World War II irreversibly changed U.S. society and laid the basis for a renewed rise of struggles for women's emancipation. $14.95

SEE FRONT OF BOOK FOR ADDRESSES

The Rise and Fall
of the Nicaraguan Revolution

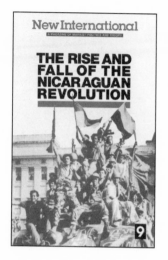

SOCIALIST WORKERS PARTY RESOLUTIONS AND ARTICLES BY JACK BARNES, STEVE CLARK, AND LARRY SEIGLE
Lessons for fighters everywhere from the workers and peasants government that came to power in July 1979. Based on ten years of journalism by working-class activists from inside Nicaragua, this special issue of *New International* magazine recounts the achievements and worldwide impact of the Nicaraguan revolution. It then traces the political retreat of the Sandinista leadership that led to the revolution's downfall at the end of the 1980s. Includes the "Historic Program of the FSLN." $14.00 Also available in Spanish in *Nueva Internacional* no. 3.

Sandinistas Speak

Speeches, Writings, Interviews with Leaders of Nicaragua's Revolution
TOMÁS BORGE, CARLOS FONSECA, DANIEL ORTEGA, AND OTHERS.

The best selection in English of historic documents of the FSLN, and speeches and interviews from the opening years of the 1979 Nicaraguan revolution. Includes "Nicaragua: Zero Hour" by FSLN founder Carlos Fonseca. $16.95

The Grenada Revolution

The Second Assassination of Maurice Bishop

by Steve Clark

The lead article in *New International* no. 6 reviews the accomplishments of the 1979–83 revolution in the Caribbean island of Grenada. Explains the roots of the 1983 coup that led to the murder of revolutionary leader Maurice Bishop, and to the destruction of the workers and farmers government by a Stalinist political faction within the governing New Jewel Movement.

Also in *New International* no. 6: Washington's Domestic Contra Operation *by Larry Seigle* • Renewal or Death: Cuba's Rectification Process *two speeches by Fidel Castro* • Land, Labor, and the Canadian Revolution *by Michel Dugré.* $15.00

Maurice Bishop Speaks

The Grenada Revolution and Its Overthrow, 1979-83

Speeches and interviews by the central leader of the workers and farmers government in the Caribbean island of Grenada. $24.95

Distributed by Pathfinder

U.S. Imperialism Has Lost the Cold War . . .

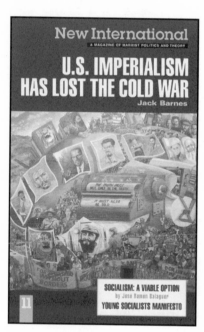

. . . That's what the Socialist Workers Party concluded a decade ago, in the wake of the collapse of regimes and parties across Eastern Europe and in the USSR that claimed to be Communist. Contrary to imperialism's hopes, the working class in those countries had not been crushed. It remains an intractable obstacle to reimposing and stabilizing capitalist relations, one that will have to be confronted by the exploiters in class battles—in a hot war.

Three issues of the Marxist magazine *New International* analyze the propertied rulers' failed expectations and chart a course for revolutionaries in response to the renewed rise of worker and farmer resistance to the economic and social instability, spreading wars, and rightist currents bred by the world market system. They explain why the historic odds in favor of the working class have increased, not diminished, at the opening of the 21st century.

New International no. 11

U.S. Imperialism Has Lost the Cold War *by Jack Barnes* • Socialism: A Viable Option *by José Ramón Balaguer* • Young Socialists Manifesto $14.00

New International no. 10

Imperialism's March toward Fascism and War *by Jack Barnes* • What the 1987 Stock Market Crash Foretold • Defending Cuba, Defending Cuba's Socialist Revolution *by Mary-Alice Waters* • The Curve of Capitalist Development *by Leon Trotsky* $14.00

New International no. 7

Opening Guns of World War III: Washington's Assault on Iraq *by Jack Barnes* • 1945: When U.S. Troops Said "No!" *by Mary-Alice Waters* • Lessons from the Iran-Iraq War *by Samad Sharif* $12.00

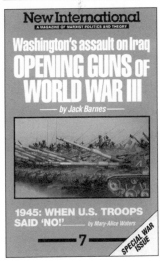

Distributed by Pathfinder

These issues of **New International** are also available in the Spanish **Nueva Internacional**, the French **Nouvelle Internationale**, and the Swedish **Ny International**.

THE RUSSIAN REVOLUTION

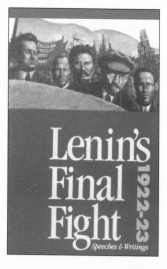

LENIN'S FINAL FIGHT
Speeches and Writings, 1922–23
V. I. Lenin

In the early 1920s Lenin waged a political battle in the leadership of the Communist Party of the USSR to maintain the course that had enabled the workers and peasants to overthrow the tsarist empire, carry out the first successful socialist revolution, and begin building a world communist movement. The issues posed in Lenin's political fight remain at the heart of world politics today. 19.95

THE FIRST FIVE YEARS OF THE COMMUNIST INTERNATIONAL
Leon Trotsky

During the early years of the Communist International, from 1919 through 1922, its course was recorded in reports and resolutions shaped above all by its central founding leader, V.I. Lenin, as well as by Leon Trotsky. This two-volume collection contains speeches and writings by Trotsky on the struggle for working-class power in the imperialist epoch, the worker-peasant alliance, the fight for national liberation, defense of the Soviet republic, and much more. In two volumes, price of each is $25.95.

ALLIANCE OF THE WORKING CLASS AND THE PEASANTRY
V.I. Lenin

From the early years of the Marxist movement in Russia, Lenin fought to forge an alliance between the working class and the toiling peasantry. Such an alliance was needed to make possible working-class leadership of the democratic revolution and, on that basis, the opening of the socialist revolution. $17.95

THE HISTORY OF
THE RUSSIAN REVOLUTION

Leon Trotsky

The social, economic, and political
dynamics of the first socialist
revolution as told by one of its central
leaders. "The history of a revolution is
for us first of all a history of the
forcible entrance of the masses into
the realm of rulership over their own
destiny," Trotsky writes. Unabridged
edition, 3 vols. in one. $35.95

THE THIRD INTERNATIONAL
AFTER LENIN

Leon Trotsky

Written in 1928, this is Trotsky's alternative
to Stalin's course toward gutting the
revolutionary program of the Communist
International. "An international communist
program is in no case the sum total of
national programs or an amalgam of their
common features," Trotsky wrote. "In the
present epoch, to a much larger extent than
in the past, the national orientation of the
proletariat must and can flow only from a world orientation and
not vice versa. $25.95

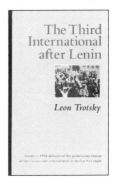

SELECTED WORKS OF V.I. LENIN

Three-volume selection includes "What Is To Be Done?,"
"Two Tactics of Social Democracy in the Democratic
Revolution," "One Step Forward, Two Steps Back," "The
Rights of Nations to Self-Determination," "State and
Revolution," "Imperialism, the Highest Stage of Capitalism,"
"The April Theses," "The Proletarian Revolution and the
Renegade Kautsky," "The Tax in Kind," "Better Fewer, but
Better," and more. $50.00

The Communist International
in Lenin's Time

To See the Dawn

Baku, 1920—First Congress of the Peoples of the East

How can peasants and workers in the colonial world achieve freedom from imperialist exploitation? By what means can working people overcome divisions incited by their national ruling classes and act together for their common class interests? These questions were addressed by 2,000 delegates to the 1920 Congress of the Peoples of the East. $19.95

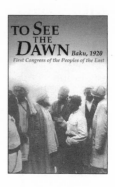

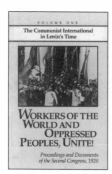

Workers of the World and Oppressed Peoples, Unite!

Proceedings and Documents of the Second Congress, 1920

The debate among delegates from 37 countries takes up key questions of working-class strategy and program and offers a vivid portrait of social struggles in the era of the October revolution. 2 vol. set, $65.00

Lenin's Struggle for a Revolutionary International

Documents, 1907–1916; The Preparatory Years

The debate among revolutionary working-class leaders, including V.I. Lenin and Leon Trotsky, on a socialist response to World War I. $32.95

Other volumes in the series:

The German Revolution and the Debate on Soviet Power (1918–1919)
Founding the Communist International (March 1919)

Available from Pathfinder